LIVING THE JOURNEY

LIVING THE JOURNEY

MY STORY AND JOURNEY OF THE UPS AND DOWNS OF LIFE

Verda Boss

JONES MEDIA PUBLISHING

Jones Media Publishing
10645 N. Tatum Blvd. Ste. 200-166
Phoenix, AZ 85028
www.JonesMediaPublishing.com

Disclaimer:

The author strives to be as accurate and complete as possible in the creation of this book, notwithstanding the fact that the author does not warrant or represent at any time that the contents within are accurate due to the rapidly changing nature of the Internet.

While all attempts have been made to verify information provided in this publication, the Author and the Publisher assume no responsibility and are not liable for errors, omissions, or contrary interpretation of the subject matter herein. The Author and Publisher hereby disclaim any liability, loss or damage incurred as a result of the application and utilization, whether directly or indirectly, of any information, suggestion, advice, or procedure in this book. Any perceived slights of specific persons, peoples, or organizations are unintentional.

In practical advice books, like anything else in life, there are no guarantees of income made. Readers are cautioned to rely on their own judgment about their individual circumstances to act accordingly. Readers are responsible for their own actions, choices, and results. This book is not intended for use as a source of legal, business, accounting or financial advice. All readers are advised to seek the services of competent professionals in legal, business, accounting, and finance field.

Printed in the United States of America

ISBN: 978-1-948382-12-0 paperback
JMP2020.2

CONTENTS

ACKNOWLEDGEMENTS

I want to express my extreme gratitude and love to;
God and Debbie Jones for the hours of work done
with me in editing my story.

The "Journey" painting by my nephew
Taylor Van Buskirk whom I call Vern.

All of the photo work my thanks goes out to
Lee Halpin and his mother Chris Halpin

* * *

In memory of Gladys Van Buskirk,
for all her love, teaching and understanding.

* * *

PROLOGUE

From Doormat to Dynamic

When I began writing, my intention was to allow my six grandchildren to know me better. This was because, as an entire family, we only get to see one another a couple of times each year. As I wrote, I realized that I was nearing the age of 50. Since my parents had passed away when they were each 50-something, I figured that I was nearing the end of my life also; so, it was more urgent for me to put my life on paper.

As I continued writing, it occurred to me that times in my childhood had touched me emotionally. My thinking was about the wonder of what was making me feel so vulnerable and tender. I wanted to know more what that was about. I verbalized, asking myself, "When was the first time that you felt so lonely?" That brought me to a lot of tears.

As I went on, my thoughts took me to another memory and yet another. My curiosity was stirred. I began to think that I needed to get to know myself. As time went by, my own story became a true learning experience for me.

One of the local hospitals in West Covina had a women's center that offered workshops. One that stood out for me was entitled "From Doormat to Dynamic." It was a 10-week, one-day-a-week program that began to open my eyes. I enrolled right away because I was still feeling pumped up and enlightened from another 10-week workshop that I had just completed, "Woman Aware and Choosing."

Over several years, I took both of those workshops a total of four times. Sober with the program of Alcoholics Anonymous (AA) almost one year when all this began, I was completely open to learning all that I could about what made me who I was.

In this same time frame, my therapist, Earl, told me about a Christian twelve-step program, Overcomers Outreach, that had just begun at a local church. The founders, Bob and Pauline, had been in AA and Al-Anon for many years when they contacted the central office of AA in New York state and, through a required and eventual process of approval, obtained permission to use the Twelve Steps. The Twelve Steps, derived from the Christian Oxford Group founded in 1922, were of great interest to me. I involved myself with that group one evening a week. The only difference between AA and the Christian group I attended was that my group identified our Higher Power as Jesus.

Coming upon all these programs just when I was ready to soak in as much as possible, I was like a sponge! I completed the third step of AA and made the decision to surrender my life over to the care of God. My entire outlook on life began to change.

As the changes continued, I realized that God is always listening! God, as I believe to be the Holy Spirit, is ever present. I can hear His whisper in my ear, especially when I am trying to decide something; and I find myself talking to that Presence as I would a constant companion. I now understand what my mother always told me, "You will develop a relationship with Jesus one day."

My response was always, "Yeah Mom," as I rolled my eyes.

I had no idea how that could happen, just as I had no idea when she explained to me when I was baptized at the age of eight, "Now that you have asked Jesus into your heart, He will be with you wherever you go." She also said, "Just remember not to take Jesus anywhere that He does not want to be."

Oh my! That was *always* on my mind when I knew that I was doing things and being in places I ought not to be according to how I had been taught when I was growing up. It always seemed so far-fetched to me. I never would have told her that I did not understand.

Now I do understand and can live my life accordingly.

I lived the first half of my life in such ignorance to how it could have been; but now I am so happy! Praise God, I got it! I have also learned how to be aware of God's presence and how to feel His leading into the right direction. I know that God is <u>always</u> listening. <u>Most</u> of the time I also know how to listen and wait for the leading that I know He wants to give.

Yes, the first 50 years of my life I spent trying to impress, get approval, and be successful materially. That resulted in a seemingly endless period of 30-plus years, the digging of a pit of despair. Conversely, for the past 30-plus years I have been writing. I find it very beneficial to my emotional, spiritual, and physical well-being. Today I believe that my story helps others to be inspired to go in search of their own purpose and share it with the world as I have here.

We all have a story!

CHAPTER ONE

Burning Desire to Tell My Story

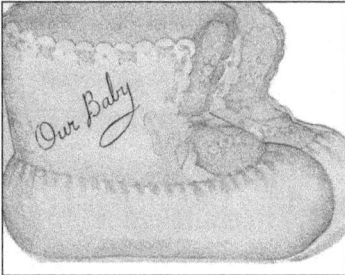
Birth announcement.

Birth announcement, interior.

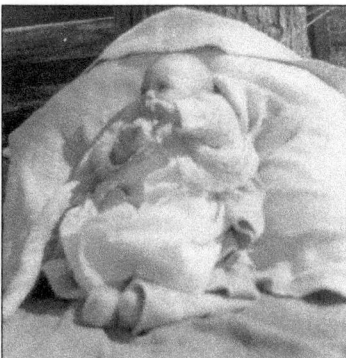
First baby picture.

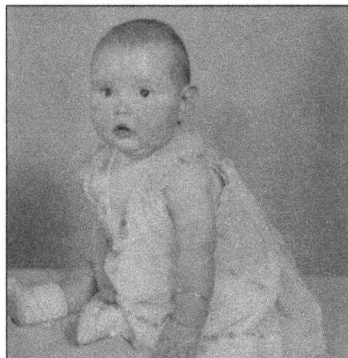
Sitting up.

Two years old.

On a stormy night in a little house behind St. Mary's hospital in Long Beach, California, I was born. The hospital itself had been structurally condemned after a big earthquake not long before. It was Saint Patrick's Day! Wouldn't I be named something fitting? The nuns, Mom told me years later, having pointed out the historical significance of the day, expressed their disapproval about her naming me "Verda."

Before I continue, let me mention that I begin most days by thanking God for the parents that He assigned to birth me. I thank God that they taught me that Jesus is the son of God, and that God is the father of all of us. Jesus, they taught me, came to teach us all how to live our lives with free spirits. I believe that God's Word was written to teach us how to live that life.

A new sister.

One year old.

New tricycle.

Our new house in Long Beach.

Our new house in Long Beach.

Our new house in Long Beach.

Off to church.

Off to church.

Dressed down.

Me and Ray's dog, Slick.

Mom, Uncle Myron, Momma D, Uncle Frank, and Uncle Clifford.

My mother was born with a heart valve that pumped the wrong way. Such an issue could be corrected at birth these days. Not then. My mother knew that she would likely not live long; however, she repeatedly risked having and wanted children enough to eventually trust God to give her healthy babies. He did just that.

Mom was ill much of the time because of her heart condition. Even as a little girl, I did what I could to help her. Strange how even very small children will feel responsible with things like that.

When I was about 3 years old, my mother became pregnant again. The doctors advised her that she was pushing childbearing too far and needed to terminate the pregnancy.

I was sent to stay with my "Momma D," as we called our maternal grandma. (Her actual name was Elsie Kemply: married name, Scovil.) I have no idea why it was Momma D, except that it was my understanding that she did NOT want to be called "Grandma" by anyone! I have some fond memories of that 3-month period of my life; however, some are not so great. For one, my mother's youngest brother, my uncle, lived with Momma D. He suffered from severe epilepsy and had seizures often, which used to scare me to death. I always liked people and never knew a stranger. Plus, Mom often mentioned that I talked with strangers at bus stops and such too often. My uncle's name was Clifford, and he loved me much, wanting to hug me or hold my hand when we walked to the corner on my way home; but my fear interfered with my feelings for him. I could not let him get very close.

My brother Ray and I were the only children in Mom's family, and all our uncles doted on us. Much in our formative years was reasonably normal.

Ray lived healthily until the age of 86, and I am now in my 80s! Still, I can not fully explain the burning desire that I have had most of my life to write about my life and my feelings.

One great memory that I have from my time with Momma D was working in the garden with her. She owned the city lot next to the one on which her home's lot was located. That second lot spanned the distance from one street to the next. The additional lot was mostly flowers. In those days, our baking flour came in printed fabric bags. From the material of those flour sacks, Momma D made quilts and sewed me little sunsuits to wear in the garden. When we were out in the garden, people often stopped to ask if they could buy a bouquet. She would reply, "Just go pick some!" I loved those afternoons!

Two blocks from Momma D, down a little dirt road, lived a pregnant lady. I kept seeing her get bigger and bigger. In those days it was known as "expecting." She was expecting and I was expecting! As I never knew a stranger, I determined to get over there and get to know her. My observation skills led me to watch until I saw diapers and baby items hanging on the clothesline. That meant a baby was in that house! I introduced myself, and I do not recall Momma D being anywhere in the vicinity when that happened. I remember admiring her baby and helping her fold diapers when I visited. This may have been my earliest awareness of loving babies and wanting to be around them. I loved babies so, I would do anything to be with that baby!

Along with spending time with that baby, I also enjoyed looking at baby pictures. We knew two missionaries, sisters known as old maids (though they were probably not yet out of their 20s) who spent much of their time in Africa. They sent me so many pictures of African babies when they wrote. I wanted to get them all and bring them to our house!

Another flower memory from being with Momma D was that annually on Memorial Day she and Mom would fill the trunk of our car with flowers, go to two cemeteries, and there place the flowers on family members' graves. The old cemetery, the first Sunnyside, on top of Signal Hill, was where all the older ancestors were buried. The more recent cemetery, with the same name then, just down the hill and a few miles to the north, was resting place to more recently deceased family members. That cemetery contained no large headstones, just flat-to-the-ground plaques.

One such visited grave was that of my mother's older sister, Florence. Both Florence and her baby had died shortly after the baby was born, during the big flu epidemic in the early 1900s. The baby was buried in the same casket as Florence, in the mother's arms, on Signal Hill. This made a great impression of sadness upon me as a little girl. I used to look with wonder at the large tombstone on their grave, thick marble etched with their names and such. On the very top of the headstone was a separate angel sculpture.

One day when we went to visit, the angel was gone. I listened as Mom and Momma D talked about how someone had taken it off—stolen it right off the top of that baby and mother's grave. They sounded so sad that it made me sad too.

Being a part of Momma D's love of flowers was only one of my strong memories of her and her artistic interests.

We did not have TV when I was growing up, so we listened to radio programs. As we listened, Momma D sat right next to the old-fashioned pot belly stove in her overstuffed chair reading the newspaper. I sat on the arm while she did that. When finished reading, she drew pictures all around the border of it. As a young lady, she was an accomplished artist and had painted many pictures. I was later told that one of them was on display in a museum in Sacramento, California. A large one hung in her bedroom. Uncle Myron (Mom's brother) later had it and promised it to me. Through the years, however, it was lost to Myron's second wife. My brother did have one in his home. How fortunate! I do now own some that Vern, my nephew, painted. He inherited the gifts of music and painting from both Momma D and my mom. I am proud of his creations!

While I was staying with Momma D, Uncle Myron and Aunt Jackie (his wife, my favorite aunt) came and took me to my own home to see Mom and Dad. I don't think that Ray was home that day; he wasn't home much. But his new puppy, a black and white bundle of fur, Slick, was! And how cute he was! I didn't know that visit had such an impact on my feelings until I started writing as an adult. When I came to that memory, I began to cry, realizing that it had had a real impact on me as a 3-year-old.

On the day that I met Slick at Mom and Dad's, the message that I received was that Ray was better than I was. I so worshipped him as my big brother. Why did he get to live at home, and I did not?

In truth, my parents could not send him away because he was in school and Dad was working two jobs. The puppy was helping keep Ray occupied as Dad was having a nurse stay with Mom while he was away. This is all reasonable in hindsight; however, the message that I picked up was that I was not good enough to get to stay home. My 3-year-old mind processed a completely different message than was intended. My first "turning point" in life happened right then. I decided that I would learn to take care of Mom so that I would never be sent away again. But for now, I was not good enough. That message replayed off and on in my head for years.

In addition, Ray was almost five years older than I was; and he did not like me tagging along with him.

Once in a while Mom said, "Oh Ray, let her go with you."

"She's too fat," he would reply, "and she whines too much!"

Ray's words then reinforced to my little mind that I was not good enough AND that I was too fat. I believed it; and for most of my life since then I have battled my weight. However, when I look at my childhood pictures objectively, there is no image of "too fat" present.

I also remember a day when I was about 7. I was walking down our driveway thinking how sad I felt and wishing that I could just lose my self-control and misbehave so that someone would make me talk about how I was feeling. My formed thought spoke in my head: Maybe I could write a book to let people know how lonely I felt.

How alone, and how sad.

I was whining in my mind.

But I was whining for a reason, as a coping mechanism. Through my early writing, I repeatedly asked myself where my low self-esteem began. Why did I allow people to be verbally abusive to me, and to tell me who I was?

Today, I have many of those answers. Adults and older siblings may not know how offhanded comments and actions can negatively impact a little one's life far into that one's adulthood.

I do know today how some affected mine. One day years ago, as my daughter and I talked about that conversation between my brother and mother, when he said that I was fat and whined—me trying to prove to her what an impact negative words can have on a person—my daughter surprised me with her words: "Mom, you still whine."

What? I examined myself and made more changes.

Today, I am pretty sure that Vicki wouldn't say that. That's because I no longer suffer from that whining which was self-pity—that feeling sorry for myself that I could not shake. I now know, from recovery and many meetings, that I have a right and the responsibility to change how I am thinking and how I behave. And I do. I am free.

CHAPTER TWO

Slippers to Church

One Sunday morning—I don't know how old I was, maybe 5—I was all gussied up in my ruffled "Shirley Temple" satin, fluffy dress. My hair was done in rows and rows of bouncy curls, with a big matching bow. Just like Momma liked. My little patent leather shoes were out, waiting for me to put them on.

I did not put them on. I had decided that I would wear my house slippers instead. I put them on. Then, I went out, got into the car, and sat to wait for the family to go to church. This was a little unusual for me, because they were usually in the car waiting for me. I thought that I was in luck; nobody seemed to notice. I sat quietly all the way; and when we arrived at church, I got out of the car with everyone else. And there I was, in my slippers. Not exactly the shoes that Mom had put out for me.

She noticed immediately. "Where are your patent leather shoes?" she asked a bit harshly.

"Oh!" I replied with a gesture of surprise, "I forgot to put on my shoes!"

She was so embarrassed, but I didn't get into any trouble as I remember.

I don't know if that was my first act of rebellion, but it stands out in my mind as a funny little thing that I did to express how I did not like having to dress up every Sunday to go to church. I would have been so happy if I could have worn a pair of my brother's Levi jeans! However, girls did not wear pants in those days.

All dressed up for San Diego Zoo.

CHAPTER THREE

My Early Years

Kindergarten

I never did like school, from the very beginning. I think I would have been a good candidate for home schooling if that had been available.

Ray and I rode the city bus, picked up about three city blocks from home, to Garfield Elementary in Long Beach. This school was an old one, and I don't have much memory of it. I do remember that at "rest time" we had a big stack of quilted-type mats to put on the floor to lie down on.

We needed to take a mat from the pile and put it somewhere in the room to lie on for our rest time. Most of the kids put their mats down in a row in an open space of the room. I always put my mat behind the piano like I thought I was hiding. I seem to recall a fishbowl of some kind back there. I usually fell asleep and had to be awakened.

At story time when the teacher read us a story, we had to sit in a circle with our legs crossed. I could not cross my legs like the other kids did. I was never able to do that, which made me feel different from the others. I never could sit up straight.

I learned later that I have a kyphosis of my spine, which has gotten worse as I have gotten older. It was commonly called a humpback or dowager's hump, and I always got downgraded for bad posture. Today children are regularly screened for this, and they can correct the problem when they are young.

Because it was a "posture" problem, my mother would have me walk around the house with heavy books on my head so I would stand up straighter to balance them.

I always had an admiration for people who had nice straight backs and felt inferior because of it. Friends speaking with me sometimes instinctively or subconsciously straighten their backs without thinking. I know they are not being critical of me, it just happens. Other than that, I have little to no memory of the first and second grades of school.

It was within this time frame that I contracted Scarlet fever and the County quarantined our home. (I had had whooping cough when I was too young to remember.) My dad and my brother went to work and school but could not enter my room. A "Quarantine" sign was placed in the front window of our home. I do remember the county nurse coming to check on me, and the neighbor kids came to my bedroom window to talk to me. I missed a lot of school and was instructed to take my temperature often, always hoping that it would be down. When the fever did finally break, my skin started peeling and looking rather creepy like crepe paper.

My dad brought me candy bars, but I couldn't eat them until I got better. I had a nice stash when I finally got well!

I also remember that once I was back at school the librarian told me quite loudly that I needed to write my whole name on one line on the library card when I checked a book out. It embarrassed me. I guess I was putting my name on two lines because I printed so big and my name was four words: Verda May Van Buskirk.

Early on in school, Ray rode his bike and I rode the city bus by myself. Sometimes I walked home, crossing a major street, Willow, with no concern. Why? Because I liked to stop and see our family friends, Harry and Beulah, on my way. They were kind of like an aunt and uncle to me. That sure could not happen nowadays. I never felt unsafe. My mother had warned me if I noticed anyone that felt strange, "Just walk into the nearest house like it is yours."

People didn't lock doors. How different it is for our kids today.

Ray had a horse named Chompo, kept down by the old Los Angeles River in a corral and pasture, about a mile away from the house. Once in a while Dad fed and watered her when my brother could not. A couple of times, when I found out that's where he was, I ran down there just so I could get a ride back in the rumbleseat in the back of his work car. I know now it was kind of a bother for him to have to open that thing up for me, but it was so fun to be able to ride back there.

One day Ray and a buddy of his were going horseback riding and I got to go along riding behind Ray, bareback. Dad thought it was dangerous for kids to ride with a saddle. I must have been about 7 years old.

We were riding along smoothly, and I felt so happy and grown up; this was a great day! Then, suddenly, Chompo jumped! She leaned left, then scooted right rapidly. And again! I was trying to hold on, then saw that Chompo had shied at a log lying along the path. Next thing I knew, I fell off. I went off the horse with my right arm straight out to catch myself, so it broke. Of course, I was immediately crying and whining for my mom. With all the noise I made, the horse took off running down the road. Ray felt bad, but he had to go after Chompo on his buddy's horse.

As he left to get Chompo, he yelled, "Don't cry and I'll give you a quarter!"

I sucked it up right away. A quarter in those days was a lot of money. (This was to be the beginning of my respect for money.)

It seemed out of nowhere that another kid showed up on the trail on his bike. I don't remember who he was, but he had a First Aid kit in a pack on his bicycle. He must have been a Boy Scout. He got his book out and was telling me I needed to bend my arm. His kit had a sling in it so I needed to bend the arm so he could tie the sling around my neck to hold my arm. The bone had slipped so that my elbow could not bend, and a big bump had formed on the inside of my right forearm. While he was "working" on me, my mother showed up.

I don't know how in the world she got the news. Maybe Ray's buddy ran to our house to tell her. She put me in the car and drove me straight to the hospital where Dr. Aldridge was waiting. How he knew to be there is a mystery to me to this day. Most people did not have phones in their homes in those days. We certainly didn't have cell phones.

Ends up I had a compound fracture. That big bump on my arm was the bone trying to come through the skin.

Third Grade

Because I had broken my right arm, I had a tough time trying to write with the left hand. This was a problem in school. The teacher often scolded me for it. "Verda May, (as I was referred to in those days) you just need to learn to use that left hand." I felt so embarrassed. I was not ambidextrous and my left hand would not work the same as the right. I was so self-conscious, and maybe also self-centered. I don't think that was even a term yet.

I was so glad to get that big ol' thing (cast) off my arm. It had gotten messy, itchy, and ugly by the end of the time that I had it on. Friends had written on it and made funny pictures. The ink in those days was with a fountain pen. Having partially dropped my casted arm in the tub and gotten it wet or damp in various ways over eight weeks, among other troubles, the ink ran together and smeared. It was messy and ugly. Once free of the cast, my arm felt so lightweight. I held it in front across my body and held it with my left hand because it felt like it was going to fly away.

As I remember, my teacher that year had adopted a little girl about my age, and the teacher invited me to her home to play with her daughter. She lived in a different part of Long Beach, and the daughter went to a different school. I thought that was nice. It felt like I was a favorite. Strangely, I can't remember their names.

New School, John Muir Elementary

No more buses. It was easy getting to school because John Muir was right on the next block from our home. All I had to do was walk a short alley and there I was, at school.

Fourth Grade

I still did not like school much at this point. The only fun time was during recess chasing boys around the playground. The new school grounds were covered with asphalt and were not like the old Garfield school with dirt playgrounds. I felt like I could run faster on it and almost catch those boys.

I liked my teacher; her name was Mrs. McCracken. She was teaching us how to write cursive; and as she showed us how to hold our pencils, I saw that she had pretty hands and nice nails. I wanted to write just like she did. I set out to make sure that my handwriting was pretty. I also decided that I wanted pretty hands like hers. Being a nail biter, this motivated me. And how did I accomplish that feat? I began painting my nails. That way, instead of biting my nails, I just peeled the polish. Most of my life I have been complimented for my handwriting and my pretty nails, partially thanks to Mrs. McCracken.

This was during World War II. We had required "blackouts" at night, which meant that we needed dark covers over our windows so that no light could show through to the outside. One such morning when I got to school all the kids were talking about the "air raid" over Long Beach the night before and running around picking up shrapnel strewn across the school playground.

My parents later that day told me that they were so relieved that I had slept right through it. I was such a nervous little kid that everything scared me that appeared to be any kind of violence or disturbance. I still avoid any kind of violence!

And that event is all I now remember about that school.

I do remember during that time riding the city bus to my piano lesson every week. My piano teacher was an "old maid" lady named Miss Nelson (probably no more than 40 years of age, actually). She looked every bit like what may have described an old maid in those days. She had a large nose and was tall and skinny, with her hair drawn back into a bun at the back of her neck. She had no style. Miss Nelson always wore a rather long gray, black, or dark brown dress; usually a thin belt around her thin waist; and always old black, tie-up, block-heeled shoes and thick stockings, of course. I think she had a mole or something similar on her face. (I'm not positive about the mole, but it would have been fitting!)

Miss Nelson would sit to the side of me with a ruler and smack my hands every time I let my hand drop at the wrist or did something wrong, which seemed way too often to me. I took those darn lessons from age 3 until I was almost 8!

Miss Nelson was also the pianist at our church. I think every kid in that "big old church" as we called it, took lessons from her. I thought that they all played better than I did at our recitals. Of course, everyone told me that I did well. I was always a slow reader, so the music books were no different pace for me. However, I was able to memorize fairly easily, and I did a pretty good job on the pieces I memorized; it just felt like the others were better. I know now that I had poor eye/hand coordination. I learned that when I was over 50 years old.

Our mother was self-taught and was so wanting us to have lessons. Ray never learned to play well either. He did pick up the steel guitar for a bit, but never followed through. His son later did develop his musical talents and plays to this day. Neither Ray nor I had our mom's entertaining, musical, artistic talents. I did like to sing, and she volunteered for me to sing any time an opportunity arose to be the "special music" for a group. I know that I had an exceptionally strong voice with deep volume; but being up there in front of a group was something I just was not able to do. My stage fright was overwhelming. One time I got up there and started to sing and nothing would come out. I had to restart a couple times and I was so embarrassed. Mom said it was just stage fright and I would overcome it. Well, I never did; and I still cannot play the piano worth a darn.

CHAPTER FOUR

Vacations

Women began wearing pants during the Second World War, when they began doing men's jobs while our men were out fighting for our freedom. Back then we were singing the "Rosie the Riveter" song.

I can remember the first time my mother wore pants. We were going on vacation to Trabuco Canyon in Orange County, California; and she had bought some new pants that were similar to bib overalls, made for women. The color was a dull, forest green. My mother was not a pants kind of woman, but a hat and gloves lady. Rather than flats, Mom even wore short-heeled shoes with bobby socks to clean house.

Dad always planned our vacations way ahead of time with reservations made for cabins in different mountain areas. A few years in a row we went to Yosemite. Our tent cabin front ceiling flap extended over the existing wooden floor platform back to canvased walled enclosure which covered the cot beds when its large flapped "doors" were tied back. The ceiling also extended beyond to cover the table and chairs. Even the linens were provided. Dad always placed his cot on the outside where the table was. He put a bucket next to him with a flashlight. If a bear came, he could bang the flashlight on the bucket to scare the bear away. Our tent cabin was right across the little roadway from the Merced River the first several times we went there.

Trabuco Canyon, Ray and Verda at the water pump.

Mom's Bible group.

Hunters Lodge, driveway to the cabin.

Our tent cabin.

In the 40s, people were still doing "firefalls" off Glacier Point, which towered about 3,200 feet above the Valley. The sight was as pretty from the top as it was from the bottom in Camp Curry. One trip, we drove up to the top to experience spectating the event. That was as spectacular as watching from below because of all the red sparks flying high into the air!

All day the park rangers would light and burn a large bonfire on the edge on top of Glacier Point, until nothing was left but red coals. A large group of people always gathered there to listen to the rangers' talk about the park's history, including stories about when the Native Americans lived there, and then to watch the fire. Following is how it played out:

As darkness fell a park ranger appeared in Curry Village, below, holding a megaphone. A ranger above did likewise. First came a shout from below to above, "Hello, Glacier Point!" It echoed through the canyon.

In response was called, "Hello, Camp Curry!"

From down below came the question, "Is the fire ready?"

"The fire is ready!" was yelled down.

Then the ranger below would command, "Let the fire fall!"

And down it came! The glowing embers were poured over the edge in a steady, controlled manner. "Fire falling" resulted in a glittering cascade of red coals, like a waterfall off the face of the mountain. Pictures of the famous mountain still boast black stains from those firefalls! It was so beautiful.

Those vacations occurred shortly after the war ended in the early 1940s and at a time in Mom's life when she was not so ill. I remember that as a happy time in my life.

Mom always found a church for us to attend on Sunday wherever we were. Since it was vacation time and most were informal services happening outside, I didn't have to be all dressed up. Another reason to like summer vacations! As for Mom, I do not think that she ever wore pants after that first year.

Birthday friends—age 10.

CHAPTER FIVE

Our Move to Cypress, Fifth Grade

It was the summer of 1945, if I am correct. We moved out to Orange County to the ranch for which my dad had longed for most of his life. It was a 10+ acre property with an old, rundown house on it. My mother was not real happy about this; but for Dad's sake she agreed to sell our brand new house that they had bought in Long Beach a couple years before WWII to move out to the country where Dad so wanted to have some livestock and land.

Mom was much a city girl and loved the "cosmopolitan" (as she called it) kind of life. Recall with me that her form of dressing down was to wear bobby socks with her older high heels on, to clean house. Now we were buying this old run-down house and a half-built barn out in a different county away from all her friends. Mine too, by the way. But I am a country girl at heart and don't remember it being that big a deal for me.

Mom and Momma D got busy cleaning up the old place. They even brought in a garden hose to begin the cleanup. This house had been used as a daycare center in its previous life in some other city, then moved to the ranch land. It boasted a sunroom down the west side; and all the windows had bars like a wooden ladder running across horizontally, maybe to keep kids from the windows. The house had been placed on a high foundation and finished with what was at that time a shingle that was to last a lifetime. It's possible that it was moved there by Mr. Draper, the man from whom Dad bought it.

After hosing it down, Mom and Momma D continued the transformation by wallpapering. An old wood stove provided heat, which was what Momma D had at the time; so, to her it was no big deal. It was to my mother. Later, Dad replaced the wood stove with a large floor furnace. At first the entire place was pretty makeshift, but Mom made it into a real home. She was good at that. Later, Dad also built a large addition on the back—consisting of a laundry area and another bedroom. Prior to that, the wringer washing machine was outside at the back of the kitchen.

One day, as it poured outside, I watched out the kitchen window. I felt sorry that the cows couldn't be in shelter, dry and warm as I was. I told my mother about my concern.

She said, "Look at them, Verda Mae. Their rumps are to the rain, and their heads are down. God gave them the sense to avoid the rain and weather the storms."

Sometimes a few simple words from her were all that I needed to accept circumstances and see the positive.

Dad loved that ranch-house from Day 1. He set about putting in fencing around the entire 10-acre property. Having found a great deal on used split railroad ties and barbed wire that he bought at the secondhand salvage supply store, he built corrals and pens for his livestock. And then I knew beyond any doubt that our animals were able to withstand the storms they encountered.

Dad worked full time at the Shell oil refinery in Wilmington; and then in Dominguez, California, which was probably 20 miles or more away. In Long Beach we had lived fairly near his work. Still, he was happy as could be and didn't mind the drive. He began going to the weekly auction on Saturdays and buying a calf here and a hog there. We had chickens, rabbits, guinea hens, dogs, a cat, pigs, cattle, and a horse. With a sign placed out by the road, Mom sold eggs for 50 cents a dozen. Dad planted all kinds of fruit trees and a veggie garden. Mom and Momma D put in flower beds all around the house. And this truly became home.

Ours was one of the larger acreages in the area, a long and narrow piece of land. A streetcar rail called the "red car" trekked across the back, running from the old downtown of Santa Ana to downtown Los Angeles (LA). That was a modern commuter in those days.

The two plots to the east of us were probably about two acres each, and east of them was a large vegetable farm of maybe 30 or more acres. An old shack on that property was home for a Mexican family. They had no bathroom and a bunch of kids; they just used an old outhouse. A big, galvanized metal tub sitting on a fire ring heated water every Saturday for their baths. I felt sorry for them, but they were a happy family. When their papa came home from work, they all ran out to greet him and carry his lunch pail. He always had a little treat for them in that lunch box. I thrilled to watch their extreme happiness.

I loved to visit there and "help" by watching their mom cook Mexican food. I had never eaten Mexican food before then. One day, she gave me a dish of enchiladas to take home. It was what we would today call stacked enchiladas: layered tortillas with I don't remember what all, with cheese. I have loved Mexican food ever since.

The two smaller places to the east of our house had smaller houses of the same era, style, and finish; kind of in line with ours, off the road on their separate land parcels. Come to think about it, maybe Mr. Draper had moved them on those small properties and sold them separately.

Next to our place lived an older couple from England by the name of Sherock. He had homing pigeons that he let out every day. They would fly all around; and then when they returned, he fed them. The Sherocks were a short, funny couple. She was tiny and kind of wiry. It was like her whole purpose was to keep old Fred happy. He was a chubby fellow with wild white hair, unshaved most of the time. I wish I could remember her name. You would think I would, because he was always yelling for her to do or bring him something.

About once a month he took his birds way out somewhere and turned them loose, then tried to beat them home. Most of the time the birds won. One day I got to ride with him; I thought it was fun to see if we could win.

On the east side of the Sherock home was the Taylor family. They had three boys; and their little house was a two-story white wood frame, just like ours. I don't remember ever being in their house. The middle son was Leon, and he was in my same class. Cypress Elementary School had only one room for each school grade; we had about 20 to 25 kids in the class. Leon and I were both starting at that school in the fifth grade.

I was 10 years old, a bit chubby, and in an awkward stage. I remember one day I was feeling so fat that I put on one of my mother's girdles. I did not know to take the clip garters off. The garter is what Mom hooked to her stockings to hold them up. I got up out of my desk and was walking to the teacher's desk and one of those garters fell off on the floor. I was so embarrassed.

In those days they didn't make or sell bras for young girls, and I felt like I needed one because of my chubbiness. My mother took one of her brassieres and altered it to fit me. My mother had very large breasts, so had her brassieres custom-made at a specialty store in downtown Long Beach. She had to adjust a lot for me. Looking back at my pictures, I wasn't nearly as chubby as I felt. Most girls my age did not wear bras. One day a boy ran past me and snapped the back of my bra: another big embarrassment for me, I was so self-conscious and awkward.

Verda, age 11.

That's about all I remember about the first year of my life on the ranch. I am still in touch with two classmates from my fifth grade. They are Joe and Delores. They were both raised on a dairy farm there in Cypress, and when they graduated from high school they married. Joe's father passed away when we were in the sixth or seventh grade, and he had to work the dairy for his mom and sister after that. They were part of the Portuguese community in our area. There were the Dutch dairies and the Portuguese dairies.

Joe and Delores did very well for themselves and now travel in a large RV; and when they come down to Arizona, they usually give me a call. I happily drop everything to go meet them for lunch because their friendship is important to me. They are a special couple.

In the 5th grade at Cypress Elementary, my teacher's name was Mrs. Listener, as I remember. The school was typical of the time, but what I would now call a beautiful, old building with high ceilings and huge tall windows to the outside. We each had a desk with a seat that folded down and was attached to the desk behind. Each had a shelf for our books under the top and an ink well hole on the upper corner. Many of those old schools are historic buildings now.

The little town was very small, hardly on the map; with the railroad track at its east end and the road continuing into farmland and orchards. There were no traffic lights, as I recall. However, there was a stop sign just west of the school, which was a few blocks from the hardware/lumber yard. The town also boasted a corner drugstore with a soda fountain, post office, and some miscellaneous buildings and the Sorghum Mill. Once you got across the tracks it was the end of the town. If it wasn't for that stop sign, a person would drive right through and not notice they had gone through a town.

By eighth grade, I had talked my parents into allowing me to go with my friends to a New Year's party at the little volunteer firehouse behind the lumber yard. It was at that party that I learned that people celebrate New Year's by going around kissing everyone!

Also by eighth grade, instead of having lunch in the cafeteria all the time, my friends and I would walk down to the corner drugstore and get lunch at the soda fountain counter. Our boundaries were enlarging.

Our eighth grade graduation was with a cap and gown and simulated a high school graduation. We were a rural agricultural area, so for those kids who had to go to work on the farms and not go on to high school, this graduation was it! I thought they were the lucky ones.

CHAPTER SIX

Smart and Arrogant

I was a smart aleck. That's what I knew then. If I had to now analyze my teen self and give a title, it would be: "My Passive-Aggressive, Rebellious Teen Years—An Angry Young Girl." Looking back I can see that I displayed some very rebellious actions. After graduating the eighth grade at Cypress Elementary School, I next went to Anaheim Union High School, a small-town school. This was before Disneyland existed. People often asked me where Anaheim was. Yes, Disneyland put the town on the map in 1955.

Looking back on those years, I see that I was an angry kid though I never even felt it at the time. I was watching my mother's health decline and her getting weaker, something that I could not stop. I was overweight and counting my calorie intake while, in my opinion, I watched my friends being footloose, as much as teenagers could be in our era. I felt restricted from the freedom of frivolity, and it felt unfair.

I desperately wanted to be free of the worry I was living with, and I thought that if I could be married all would be different. I wanted to have someone to hold on to. That was to be something like jumping from the frying pan into the fire. I now know that at that age I was not able to process well enough to make a good decision. At the time, though, it seemed like a reasonable solution to my 15-year-old mind.

Since I was about 12 years old, with the help of my dad, I cooked our meals and did the family laundry. I loved cooking and was pretty good at it. Dad always had a lunch pail to carry his lunch in to work. He enjoyed cookies and cake, and I was able to bake both from scratch, as they call it now, without any recipe. I also loved eating them.

At the age of 13 I weighed 130 pounds and continued gaining, to the point that I started having elevated blood pressure and a thyroid problem. I had to undergo some testing. Dr Morris put me on a thyroid pill and gave me a 1,000-calorie diet to follow.

In 1948 no such thing as "diet foods" existed. I was given a calorie chart and a way to make a substitute spread to serve as butter and mayonnaise: whip eggs with mineral oil until thick, the consistency of very soft butter. The mineral oil leaked into my panties a bit, which felt embarrassing, but I surely was not about to let anyone know. That was my little secret.

I began to lose weight, which made everything worth it to me. I pretty much stayed on my diet for three years. I had been told long before, by Dr. Morris, that I ought never to upset my mother, that that could kill her. I certainly never wanted to upset her as she was a good mom. Still, inside I felt angry. All my skinny friends were eating things that I could not have.

A small mom-and-pop store stood across the street from the school. After class, everyone walked over to buy snacks. While my friends purchased items like fudgesicles, ice cream cups, and candy bars, I handed over coins for gum. Gum contained few calories.

As we walked back to the school over the crosswalk, cars kindly stopping for us, we paid no mind. What I mean is, we walked across as slowly as possible, to make the drivers wait. I'm not sure who started that. I do know that it was one of my many rebellious acts. We were fortunate that no one tried to or even accidentally did hit us. When I see kids do that now, I find it extremely annoying. Before I let that feeling go too far, I recall how I was at that age.

Smart-Alecky Teen

I chose to take the home economics classes of sewing and cooking in my freshman year. I figured that since I already did those activities at home the classes would be easy for me. I was never a good student and always looked for the easy way to get through.

One day I entered cooking class chewing my gum, another rebellious teen moment. The rule was: Do not chew gum in class. My teacher, Mrs. Barbara Walker, called me a "gum-chewing hussy"! I took that statement straight home to my mother, who suggested that I go back and speak to the principal or counselor. It made me nervous, but I did just that.

I am sure that they let Mrs. Walker know about that; maybe that was why she never seemed to care much about me or my ability to cook. Later, in my yearbook, I noted the following message: "Were you always so sleepy? Barbara Walker, "MRS." I must have been calling her by her first name.

I did sleep a good deal in many of my classes. I also slept on the bus going to school and heading home. I thought that I was just lazy. "Fibromyalgia" was not a thing.

At the age of 60 I was diagnosed by a specialist who told me that I had most likely had this since childhood. Symptoms include body pain all over, chronic fatigue, and irritable bowel syndrome. I now also know that I was struggling with depression, also a symptom of fibromyalgia.

Back then, through it all, I sought the easy way to do any task. My mother unknowingly called it "laziness and slovenliness," Biblical terms. This just contributed to my low feelings of self-worth. I tried so hard to "not be that."

In my sophomore year I decided to take General Shop. I always liked to work outside with my dad. He could build anything and was always keeping himself busy outdoors. Sometimes he just pulled nails out of old wood that he would use for building later. Dad had many old coffee cans full of used nails.

Trying to sign up for the class was when I learned that girls did not take a "boys'" class. What?!? I took that straight to the principal and maybe my counselor. The message was verified: Shop is a boys' class; no girls are in that class. Well, I asked my best girlfriend, Sherry, to sign up. I also asked several others, one being Shirley. With so many girls now wanting the class, we were able to get in! We had had to fight for it, and I was proud that I had accomplished what I wanted to do.

We all learned how to use many power tools. We made items with wood, and we learned basic electrical and plumbing repairs. I never slept in that class; I loved doing things like that! Still, my rebellion was also disrespectful to that teacher. I would say, "Howard, is this...?" and "Howard, how is that?" I also called him Howard in a flirty way; but he just laughed with me.

That best teenage friend, Sherry, and I are still in touch. We were talking not long ago about how we have both used those shop skills in our homes. I wish now that I could apologize to that teacher, he was such a nice man.

Smart-Ass Driver

Ray had a really great hot rod: the body of a 1928 or 1929 chopped Ford, no fenders. He painted it metallic blue. I just thought that that car was something else! I wanted him to let me drive it and always asked if I could. No!

Each time I asked, Ray reminded me that a couple of years prior he had had a Model A, when I had not really known much about driving an old car. True.

Before custom job.

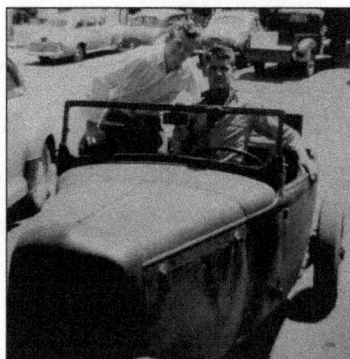

Ray and his buddy, hot rod partial.

Ray had been out helping Dad do something on the ranch, and I had decided that I was going to drive that car over to his friend Doris' house, down around the corner. As I headed quickly down our dirt road to get to the street, I tried shifting gears. Uh-oh. Unsuccessful. Those gears grinded and made a terrible sound, which Ray heard.

Did I stop, though? No, I kept going; and eventually I made it to her house, despite the noises. I don't remember if Ray ran after me or what happened. I do know that he told me that I had stripped a gear and that he would have to fix the entire transmission. In fact, he eventually customized it into a real hot rod. So, NO; I could NOT drive the hot rod!

Drag Racing

It was early 1950. Ray was overseas in the Korean War. His ship was a destroyer, the USS Rogers, which stationed in San Diego, California, when they were in port.

One weekend when the ship was in port, Ray came home on leave. Long acting older than his age anyway, Ray seemed to have grown up even a bit more. He was this weekend headed to Long Beach Junior College to see if he could meet a girl. This was not just any girl.

On another time "scouting" the campus for girls, Ray had met Joyce. He had then visited her on campus a few times when in town. And he fell in love. Joyce was quite pretty, and Ray could not stop talking about her. Because she was so classy, Ray was also afraid that she would not want to ride in an old hot rod. Therefore, before Ray asked Joyce out, he sold the hot rod and bought a nice 1947 Ford Club Coupe. Ironically, when Joyce learned what Ray had done, she expressed disappointment; she would have preferred the hot rod! Oh well. The new car was nice also.

I had also continued to enjoy cars and driving. I do not remember if in this next instance Ray had gone out to sea again, but I did have my license. I was 14 years old at the time. This was because Dr. Morris had written that I needed my license so that I could run errands and be available for my mother in case of emergency. I frequently picked up bunches of my girlfriends in the family 1948 Plymouth sedan. We then headed to church, school, or anywhere that we could find bunches of boys.

Church girlfriends.

Our youth group, led by my mother, grew as kids from Excelsior High (in which school district our church was located) got word of the group. This included my meeting Donna, who soon became a best friend. Along with her came a bunch of girls, which soon translated to a new bunch of boys! Eventually, our group was larger than the little church itself had ever been! After church we usually piled into the car to check out who might be hanging out at the drive-in. From school, we sometimes headed to Fullerton High School during lunch to meet boys. Of course, we did not know what a seatbelt was as they had not yet been invented. I became pretty popular due to my driving ability. Sometimes six or seven girls were in the car with me, sitting on one another's laps.

One evening I had my brother's '47 Coupe. I do not know how I managed that. We were packed in that thing! At some point, one of the girls we picked up mentioned that the guys were out on Ball Road drag racing. Maybe it was Shirley referring to her brother, Tom. I had had a crush on Tom since fifth grade, when Shirley and I met. So, we headed for Ball Road! Next thing I knew, we were in the race. Most likely, it happened on a dare.

Ball Road was way out in the country, where you could see headlights coming for a mile. My best thinking at the time was, "Why not?"

I remember that I was shaking and excited all at the same time. I do not know how many girls were in that car with me, all saying, "Let's do it! Verda, you can do it!"

Okay, here we are on a two-lane country road; and I'm out to beat the other guy. The guy driving right next to me. And I'm driving faster than I can ever remember. If I remember right, I chickened out at the time that we hit nose to nose. I think I got scared enough at that moment to back out.

Oh my gosh! My mom's prayers were surely with me when I was out there doing the many things that I did. By the way, Ball Road became a main street that ran across the back of Disneyland in Anaheim!

* * *

Not too long ago that best friend, Donna, sent me an email containing pictures of some old '50s cars. She wrote, "I remember a friend of mine had a bright yellow 1950 Studebaker two-door, and we were driving down Pioneer Boulevard. There were cones out in the road. Seems like my friend knocked them all over the road. On purpose..."

I did that! And I had forgotten all about it. I went right down the road tipping the edge of the cones and looking in the rearview mirror, watching them fly all over. It was those kinds of "acting out" behaviors that were mine. Married, and just a junior, my husband and I had just bought that car. (Yes, the "how-we-met" story is coming!) This little Studebaker was a two-door; it looked the same in the front as in the back. People often said, "I can't tell if you are coming or going!"

* * *

By that time, I had transferred to Donna's high school, Excelsior High, in Norwalk, Los Angeles County, California. I can't remember if I wore out my welcome at Anaheim or if I simply thought that I would be better off in a new place.

Donna was active at school, cheerleading and being involved in various clubs and groups. School started in September with the gift of a whole new group of friends. As Donna was popular and I was her friend, I was somewhat in. I liked that. I continued doing poorly academically, however.

Therefore, about halfway through that year, Excelsior suggested that I drop out; they were losing money on me due to lack of attendance. Finally, I had a reason to **not** go to school.

I followed the suggestion.

CHAPTER SEVEN

The Storm

It was the middle of the night. I was in my early teens. And, I was home alone. Or so I thought. I don't recall where my parents were; they rarely went anywhere without me.

We lived out in the country, and our door was never locked. Back then, as with many homes of that era, my bedroom was just off the living room. I was sleeping. Suddenly, loud pacing and swearing from the living room woke me! Someone was in there, crashing back and forth! And then, even more and louder profanity!

I stepped out of my room in my long, flannel nightgown, half-awake as I heard the intruder ranting, "Where the hell is Ray?"

I heard myself reply, "I don't know. He was supposed to go back to the ship in San Diego."

"Yeah, and I'm here to pick him up. I'm driving, and we're late!" He continued with some colorful Navy language, the only kind he knew, I later learned.

Through some sleepy (on my part) conversation we determined that Ray must have taken off without him. Oddly though, Ray's car was still in the driveway.

The loud, angry guy left as quickly as he had come. I went back to bed. In what seemed like seconds, another loud, angry guy was yelling at me. This time it was my brother stressfully proclaiming that it was past time for "Stonnie" to pick him up and that he needed me to drive him to "the Circle" in Long Beach so that he could then hitchhike back to "Dago!"

Huh?! I explained that Stonnie had come and gone. How could Ray have not heard all the noise that Stonnie had made right next to his room, which was really just separated by an archway covered by a drape for privacy? My brother was definitely angry. Well, how could Ray have overslept any longer than he did?

I was pretty young, so young that I don't believe that I even had a license to drive. "The Circle" that Ray referenced was a traffic circle in Long Beach that connected the Pacific Coast Highway (the 101 or "PCH") to a few other main streets heading north or south through Long Beach, California. "The Circle" was where guys often hitched rides to San Diego. And, it was somewhere between ten and fifteen miles from our home.

"No!" I said.

I did not want to get in trouble. I told Ray that. And we argued, with Ray telling me that he would get in BIG trouble if he did not get back to the ship. It must have been 2:00 or 3:00 a.m. Monday morning by that time. Of course, eventually we both got in his car and drove hastily off.

On the way back, all by myself, I felt very afraid. Not afraid of the drive itself, just afraid that I was going to get caught. I was likely only 13 at the time. It was to be the beginning of many more furious drives and frightened times.

Oops, a dent!

It was nearly a year later in June or July 1949, at Ray and Joyce's wedding, that I met Stonnie again. By then I had developed quite a bit, especially physically. I was looking older than my age and happy about it. And, amid their happiness I dreamed and thought that I had found my own. Why? Because this time Stonnie was flirting with me! I really grabbed on to that attention. I admit that I was flirting right back.

Stonnie had a girlfriend at the time, yet he started hanging out with my brother at our house even more on weekends when they had shore leave. These "liberties" were either 24- or

72-hour periods off base. Eventually, the girlfriend broke up with him. I did not have enough life experience to question why.

I think that my mother picked up pretty quickly that something was going on between Stonnie and me. She soon informed him that if he wanted to see me he needed to pick me up on Sunday mornings and attend church with me. As I look back on it, I think that Mom thought that requirement might discourage his infatuation. No, he rather may have taken it as a challenge. Maybe. I am not sure. What I am sure of is that I was "falling in love" with this attention that I was receiving. What young 14- or 15-year-old girl wouldn't fall for a good-looking guy 18 or 19 years old and in the Navy?

But Mom obviously was not falling for it. She did not care much for this guy and his fast-moving manipulation. Soon, Stonnie asked me if I would "go steady" with him? I told him that he needed to talk to my dad.

This proved no problem for smooth Stonnie, who quickly seemed to have become a buddy with my dad. He showed up often and just helped Dad outside working or with other chores. Major manipulator that he was, this worked to his advantage. Still, Mom was not so unaware of his tactics. Stonnie was taking me to church, however; and I guess that Mom was maybe thinking that his attendance there might effect some change in his fast-talking attitude.

Reviewing it all, I think that my mother simply did not have the physical or mental strength to outwit this guy; and I was too starry-eyed to think straight. Actually, which 15-year-old can think sensibly? Ah, but almost every one of us thinks that he or she can!

When we went out some place, like to a drive-in movie or one of the local drive-in diners where "all" the kids hung out for a cherry coke or cherry phosphate, it never ended there. Stonnie and Verda always ended up at the dead-end road down Acacia Street, near Coyote Creek Bridge, known for being "the place" to make out. Yep, the dead-end road...

Needless to say, but I feel that I must, it was not long before I lost my virginity. In the back seat of that dark green 1946 Mercury Club Coupe.

And when we went back to my family's home, his arm innocently placed around my shoulder, Stonnie stopped at the back door and gave me a short kiss. He always did this right after stopping mid-yard and "taking a leak." This felt awkward each time, but I did nothing about it. I still can not understand why I saw not one of the red flags flying high all around me. I guess too many stars gleamed in my own eyes. So many antics taking place so fast, along with the ever-present thought, pushed to the back of my mind, that my mom could die any day and I should not upset her.

Early on, Stonnie had taken me to meet his parents and the rest of his family. His mother was a large woman, probably just under 6 feet tall. His dad was a bit smaller in pounds and maybe two inches shorter. They fought all the time. And Stonnie told me about an instance wherein his mother, when they were all younger, picked up his dad by the front of his clothes and put him against the wall for some unknown reason. But highly likely that it was because she was angry, again!

Another story that he told me about was how, one night at the dinner table, she got mad and poured an entire bowl of gravy in his dad's lap. They did argue all the time, it seemed; and it did not matter to them who might be present.

Once, Stonnie's mother proudly informed me that she could go the entire week without speaking to any of them. I could not imagine what it would be like, as a child, to grow up not knowing why Momma is not speaking to you.

My thinking was: *"This **poor guy** grew up with this terrible behavior! No wonder he is angry and anxious."*

The scenarios past and present were so hard for me to imagine because I had never even seen an argument between my parents. Not even harsh words or a loud voice. Once in a while there occurred a "Now Don" or a "Now Gladys" with a stronger voice, their way of expressing disagreement. Yelling at each other? Never.

A couple of months into our "courtship," Stonnie got a special liberty (he was very good at that, too). I came home from some activity with the young people's church group, the only reason I was allowed out evenings, to find him waiting impatiently, as he waited most of the time. I felt slightly guilty because I had just been sitting next to Bobby Johnson's brother as he drove me home. It wasn't the first time that I had been out with him. My mother probably knew all of this and was likely rooting for the young Johnson to win out in my life.

But what did Stonnie have for me at my ripe age of 15?

A set of rings. Very pretty, with shiny diamonds. And he had picked them out. The diamonds were small, but shiny. And the setting was unique. And they were for me. For us. Or did I just assume this? Stonnie never asked me to marry him; he told me that we were going to be married. And because of the Biblical teaching about marriage being the place for "some activities" that would not be acceptable otherwise it seemed right, or at least better. Anyway, those little diamond rings made many things okay.

I was so sure that if I loved Stonnie enough he would get to know the difference between his family and mine, that he would come to understand love and mercy. That I could love that anger right out of him. Not!

He eventually used my gentle love against me, in a VERY loud voice, "You were so sheltered and brainwashed! I am a realist. I live in a **REAL WORLD!**"

I believe now that Stonnie decided early on that no woman would ever treat him the way that his mother treated his father. He often commented that marriage is a 60/40, with the man being the 60 percent. Without taking time to even realize that a difference existed in my family's way of living harmoniously or getting to know that I was not like his mother, his attitude with me was, "Get her before she gets me!" Stonnie was what one would today call "a wounded bully." Or simply "bulldozer," as one of my later counselors claimed.

How could I have ever known his thinking? And vice versa, how could he have known mine? Now I know that we functioned with many assumptions without conversations. This was the beginning of a long, painful, and eventful segment of my life.

CHAPTER EIGHT

Blind Ignorance

One day in late summer of 1951, Stonnie mentioned needing to go to San Diego for some naval reason. As it was to be a turn-around day trip, my parents gave me permission to join him. I was 16 years old, and the city was much different from what it is today.

It was a U.S. Navy town; and everywhere one looked, up and down the streets, a sea of sailors' white hats bobbed. Where currently old ships stand tied up for museum-type tours at the west end of Broadway Boulevard, formerly war ships of all kind and size were anchored row upon row upon row. Anchored there until next maneuver. This main street that runs east and west in downtown used to be called Fleet Landing and boasted a small office-type building which housed a Navy office. And the harbor was full of ships anchored all over what I believe was called The Bay.

These ships included big tenders, large ships that were like floating supermarkets, carrying supplies for the fleets of destroyers; submarines; and other smaller ships. The tenders went along with the main ships, whether on maneuvers or out to sea, in that time to Korea. Also, there were smaller landing craft, which served as taxis for people going to and from ship and shore. Along with all those bobbing white hats walking up and down the streets during off time were all the shore boats running back and forth from ship to shore to ship. San Diego was a busy port town!

That day, Stonnie drove us from LA on PCH to San Diego. No freeway existed then. As we entered town, we passed Fleet Landing on Harbor Boulevard, which further down curved south to Mexico. Just before the curve was a ferry landing depot for ferries used to take people and their cars to Coronado Island and, of course, to the beautiful old Coronado Hotel resort. Next to the ferry landing was a very nice restaurant with a view of the water and the ferry goings and comings from San Diego to the island.

Amazingly, Stonnie turned in to that parking lot and parked!

"Let's go in," he said.

How exciting! I thought with a thrill that he had planned lunch or dinner there together. I also fleetingly wondered how he would pay for that.

Oh yes, he had planned something. But it was not a romantic meal. In the foyer, to the right before the reception desk, was an alcove containing a phone booth, as was typical in upscale restaurants in those days. Stonnie proceeded to tell me that I was about to call my mother. I was to tell her that if we did not agree to get started on a wedding he was going to take me to Tijuana, Mexico, and get married right then! This was not good.

I was so nervous being in this nice place with such a weighty command. And I so feared telling my mother those words and what it might do to her health. I was also afraid of not calling. Afraid of Stonnie's possible reaction. I dialed shaking and scarcely hid the tears and tension as I spoke to her.

"Verda May, you put Stonnie on the line right now," she commanded.

I wiltingly handed him the phone, trapped in that now tiny phone booth.

I could not hear what she said to him, but I am guessing that it was, "Stonnie, bring home my daughter right now. We will talk about it." Who knows what else she said. Whatever it was, we left the romantic restaurant of doom and headed home.

I do know that one thing we talked about back at my family's home was that if I got married before high school ended I absolutely was to finish high school. Me finishing school was not important to Stonnie. His thinking was, *"fine with me"* as by then I was struggling worse than ever in my classes. Still, I made a last-ditch effort to finish. I was not really in the game in my head by then, however. I liked the social aspects but demonstrated poor attendance. What could those teachers teach me that I didn't already know?

The second week of November changed everything further and forever.

Stonnie had been home again on a liberty for the weekend. It was Sunday evening. He informed me, "We are getting married next weekend with or without your parents, so you better tell them."

I don't think I slept a wink that night. Dr. Morris' never-fading words, "Do not upset your mother," tore through me as my body quaked from fear of Stonnie's anger and manipulating power. The next morning as I prepared to leave, I could hardly walk to the door for my shaking.

Mom was sitting in the living room reading her Bible.

Timidly, I asked, "Do you want to go to a wedding this Saturday?"

"Who is getting married?" I heard her ask.

I replied, "I am." And with that, without looking back, I walked out the door, got in the car, and drove to school, fearful of what I had done.

Just before lunch, as I was in my bookkeeping class, a messenger came into the room and pulled me aside saying, "I need to speak with you."

Oh my God! I was so afraid that I had upset my mother to that unthinkable point. I stood, grabbed my belongings, and left the classroom.

Once in the hall, the messenger said, "Your mom is in her car out on the south curb. She needs to speak with you."

I walked out, feeling some relief that she was out there and not in a hospital somewhere.

Getting in the car, I still felt so afraid. I tried for casual as I asked, "What's wrong, Mom?"

"If there is going to be a wedding this Saturday, we have work to do."

The next moments and hours remain a blur to me. I just recall being confused, and unable to express much of anything.

My mother must have talked with some friends and our pastors rather than talk to me. That's all I can guess to this day. Maybe they decided that I was pregnant, so this was the thing to do. How I wish that she had opened conversation with me. I just could not do it myself. Fear of Stonnie kept winning out.

Mom had arranged with one of her best friends, Elaine, who happened to be wealthy and lived in a large, pretty home in Long Beach in what was then called The Old Country Club Estates. The reception would be held there.

I learned this as we drove to Long Beach, where we purchased dresses for my sister-in-law, Joyce; Mom; and me.

Next, we ordered a cake at a bakery; then we went to order flowers from Mom's distant cousin, the florist.

In that one afternoon and evening, the entire wedding plan came to be. Mom was a lot tougher than Dr. Morris knew or I thought she was.

All Mom's friends made invitation calls; I contacted Stonnie and told him that he needed to get home.

We were on a time crunch to get the marriage license. As we were each under 21, we had to have our mothers go with us. Stonnie was not happy about that. We drove to LA as soon as he arrived on Friday afternoon to pick up his mom and get to the Long Beach Recorder's office before it closed. The drive there was a terrifying ride. Stonnie had already been labeled, legally, a reckless driver; and he proved it again that day! Except for God's grace in our lives, I don't think that we would have lived to tell the story!

The Wedding

We had standing room only in that little church on that Saturday evening, and Elaine's home was filled to the brim. As was our custom and with no thought to the contrary from any of my family, punch and cake were served at our reception.

Stonnie's brothers wanted to know, "Where's the booze?!" When they learned there was none, they exited, letting Stonnie know that they would be at their mom's house.

We stayed just long enough for pictures to be taken, the cake cut, and a few gifts opened. My new husband was in a hurry to leave. With little personal recall of that evening, most of my memories have been jarred through viewing our photos.

I do know that we went directly to LA, to his parents' home, for the drinks. I did not know why the alcohol was so important to them. None of them were big drinkers. It made no sense to me. Maybe to them it was considered a "no-brainer" that more than cake and fruit punch would be served at a wedding. It did not make sense to me then, but I now know that I had lived sheltered from the "worldly" world.

Our honeymoon was short: We left the party at his family's home, he drove us to a motel in Hollywood, and we spent the night there. I had never even smelled alcohol and I still doubt that he had had any; however, that is all in a fog in my memory bank today.

The following week, Sunday morning, back at my family's house, I got up from my twin bed, now shared with my husband. Time to get ready for church. Stonnie informed me that he no longer needed to go to church any more.

"You are mine now."

And that was the second part of the wild first journey of my life. I was now a married woman simply because Mom assumed that I was going to have a baby. I was too naïve and ignorant to tell her otherwise. Also, related to my behavior in the backseat of that '46 Mercury Club Coupe, because of my biblical upbringing and the fact that we were "engaged," I thought that I was obligated to marry him. How different my thinking is today!

Suddenly, I was a U.S. Navy wife, and living with Mom and Dad.

At this time, the U.S. was in the midst of the Korean War. Stonnie had been due for discharge in 1951; however, he was informed that his status was being "frozen"—that he could not be discharged. So, he shipped over for another six years to receive the money that was offered for that. That was $600. Total. And then he was sent to Korea.

One evening as part of the youth group, I attended a big tent meeting down on Lakewood Boulevard in Long Beach. There, a visiting evangelist had been speaking nightly for a week as part of a revival. When he called for "those who say yes to Christ" to make their way toward the front, I found myself clearly deciding and walking forward. That night I rededicated my life to the Lord. My eyes streamed with tears of joy. I had never meant something more than that night. I needed to tell Stonnie.

Our letters were shipped via air mail, which could take weeks or longer to arrive, depending on where his ship was. As we both wrote almost daily and the ship was moving all the time, the letters stacked up in the ship's post office until the ship came to a port. Consequently, when we received the letters, they could be as stacks at a time.

So, I wrote the news to him in my daily letter. I began living my more decided life, considering more personally what part

God was taking in it. And I awaited Stonnie's reply. When it came, about half a month later, I found myself disappointed, confused, and mildly afraid. Stonnie had replied, "You sound like you've become a fanatic. Fanatics are what I am fighting over here."

That's all I needed to stuff my decision to live for God way down in my being. I did not want to be a fanatic. I wrote nothing more about it. I soon got a job with the Pacific Telephone Company as a switch board operator. It was the summer of 1952, a really hot summer. I worked a split shift: four hours in the a.m., home for four hours, back in the afternoon.

Air conditioning was something new, found only in large corporations and the like. I had never been anywhere where there was air conditioning until that job. When I got to work, I had to put on a sweater or jacket because it was so cold. When I went out at the end of my first shift, it was like walking into an oven. In a few weeks, I got very sick. I went to the U.S. Navy doctor for it and got a big surprise.

I was pregnant.

Stonnie had told me early on that he never wanted to have kids; therefore, I did not want to tell him. He had expected that it was my job to see to it that pregnancy did not happen. The fact was that we had not used birth control consistently. I had gone to the doctor and been given a prescription for a diaphragm. Much of the time, we had not taken the time to use it.

Now I was ill with bronchitis and early pregnancy. And, mostly, fear.

Mom repeatedly asked if I had told Stonnie that I was not feeling well. I repeatedly answered her: "No."

One evening she asked again, and I again had not. "Either you tell him, or I am going to," she warned.

So, though I knew that he would be upset, I did tell him. I knew that it would have only been worse if he had come home to find me six months pregnant.

Actually, my entire young life I had dreamed of being a mother, almost to obsession. My thinking was that when Stonnie had babies he would not be able to help but love them. That was another immature thought of mine, placing the actual red flag in an imaginary heart.

To my dismay, I soon learned that Stonnie meant what he had said when he stated, "I don't want kids!"

After six months of Stonnie being overseas in ocean areas outside places like Japan, the Philippines, Korea, and Hong Kong—through his stellar fashion of manipulation, he managed to be assigned to shore duty at a base by the name of Point Mugu at Port Hueneme just out of Oxnard, California in Ventura County. Our assigned housing on the base was a Quonset hut. This home had two small bedrooms, a tiny kitchen, and a miniature living room. Rent? That was $15 per month.

Prior to my daughter's arrival, my mother had come up to help me decorate our little home. She fashioned and made curtains for our windows on those oddly curved walls.

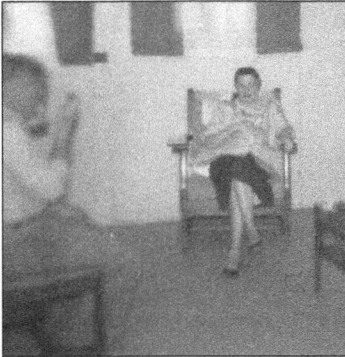
Living room.

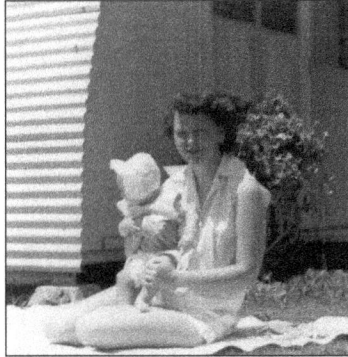
Little girl Verda and her new baby.

Mom and Dad's place.

Our new home, in process.

Vicki was born on that base in the infirmary. Stonnie dropped me off there to give birth and recover; he was pissed off because he was not allowed to stay. The cost was $5 per day to stay there, which I did for four days. One gal who worked there gave me two layettes to take home for my baby. And there

I was, scared to death of this teeny tiny baby, with no idea what I would do with her. I did have plenty of clothing for her as I had been given four showers, to make up for our lack of time for bridal showers.

One event that she and I had together in the first weeks of her life happened on a rare trip of just the two of us to Oxnard. I stopped in a coffee shop for some reason, probably to have lunch or a snack, and likely to secretly to show off my baby! I was so proud of this real accomplishment. By the way, there being no drive-throughs at the time, this was the only way to get a bite while out.

As I sat with her lying on my lap, both of us just quietly enjoying the moment, a couple from across the shop walked over. As they got quite close, the wife uttered a small gasp and asked, "Is that a real baby?"

Radiantly proud, I smiled and replied, "Yes! This is my baby!"

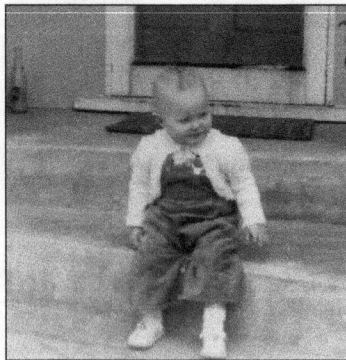

Vicki.

The husband, taking the elbow of his surprised wife, said, "Well, congratulations! We own a toy store and were admiring this little doll, wondering where she was made. We won't be asking that question today."

Yes, Vicki was a little doll! I beamed and etched the memory in my mind.

Unfortunately, the little doll's father could not see her extreme value. He had wanted a boy, and he blamed me for that not taking place. He reminded me, "I did not and do not want kids!"

To make matters worse, I got pregnant again when she was six months old. The hope of a boy had changed to the demand for another girl, because he found Vicki fun. He could toss her upside down and into the air as she stiffened and stood in reaction. But no circus act from our ten-month-old baby and no expressed hope seemed enough to keep Stonnie connected to our family. In fact, he started missing the dinner I had cooked and coming home in the early morning hours instead.

Poor baby!

I recall, still pregnant with Ric, that I accused him of having an affair.

His excuse was that he had gone to the movies. He acted incredibly insulted, "If you want to see where I am, meet me there."

The building was a shabby, old theatre where shows cost five cents for three features and the air smelled like stale cigarettes and sweat. Stonnie was not the only man spending or supposedly spending his nights there. He satisfied my doubts.

Unfortunately, that was not the only time that Stonnie was late and I was naïve about it.

A couple months later it started happening again.

He explained that I was again overreacting. "Verda, I am just learning to skate at the skating rink." That rink was named the Hippodrome, and there was actually a young woman teaching him to skate.

"Stonnie, if you're going to be that late, don't come home at all."

I now know that I was simply living in my own fantasies. I can now see that my thinking was completely unrealistic. In reality, another child only meant to Stonnie that he would have another person in his life to boss, to use, and to control.

Oddly, years later when we were living up north on a ranch in the hills (with no TV reception) going to the movies became a regular Sunday event. And then we together (with our pre-teen children) attended as many as three movies in one day. Other times the schedule looked like: church, movie, dinner, movie. And I was never the wiser about the movies themselves as I often fell asleep there, out of sheer exhaustion.

During the time that we were stationed at Port Hueneme, Dad had sold the ranch, related to my mother's ill health. He bought a nice home with a large plot of ground on Pioneer Boulevard in what was then the city of Artesia, California. Stonnie and my weekly visits there, visiting either his parents or mine, and staying at Mom and Dad's, were the glue holding together my fragile existence.

Attached to their home, between the house and the garage was a large room the size of a garage, 20' by 20'. My dad turned that into a one-bedroom apartment for our growing family as Stonnie had his shore duty transferred to Long Beach in 1953. Ric was born while we lived there. And Stonnie was again placed on a ship, the U.S.S. Magoffin (APA-199), for the remainder of his duty.

CHAPTER NINE

1955

This ought to have been a happy time as my parents had given Stonnie and me the lot at the back of the large corner property on which their home sat, on Pioneer Boulevard, for us to build our first house. Our house faced 216th Street. Being that close, I could help Dad and the lady he had hired to care for Mom. My mother was homebound and growing weaker.

My parents had always been generous toward my brother and myself as well as to the people involved in our little mission church. When Ray and his wife married, our parents gave them the down payment for their first home, in Long Beach. They also provided a home for our pastor; and when any church need arose, my parents stepped up.

Growing up in such a rigid type of faith, I knew nothing about the disease of alcoholism other than what was pointed out to me as the family drove down Ocean Boulevard now and then and Dad pointed out what we would now name "the homeless." Back then they were "alcoholics" sleeping in the doorways of old buildings.

While the contractors were building our home, my husband was overseas instructing me from each letter as to how he wanted it built. He had seen the blueprint and we then had agreed on a plan. Suddenly, he wanted our bedroom to be in the front portion of the house. That was not in the plan. I ignored these things that should have been more red flags to me.

Christmas 1955

It was December 21, 1955. I was standing at my kitchen sink doing God knows what. Was I doing the dishes? Or was I just standing there, not knowing what I was to do or how I was to feel?

Feelings were not something that I knew how to think or talk about. My plan for the day had been to decorate the tree in our home.

Just a few short hours before, as I had watched through my kitchen window and through the row of eucalyptus trees along the fence that separated our two properties, I saw my dad pull into his drive next door, get out of his car, and approach our house. I could tell by his unsteady gait that he was upset.

At that time in my life, I had long guarded myself from emotions about my mother, whether my own or others'. I did not know why. It was probably because of the knowledge of the pending doom of this day, then to come. I could not that day either allow myself to show emotion. I am sure that I did not hug him or cry. He was not crying either, though it appeared that he had been. Likely, he had been holding back to seem strong for my sake.

Earlier, Dad had walked over through the gate between our homes and told me that the injection that he had been giving Mom daily had that morning made a bubble under her skin and would not absorb. Dad knew that meant that something was not right, so he called Dr. Morris.

Dr. Morris was from the big city of New York. At that time, some doctors still made house calls for some seriously ill patients. Typically, when the doctor visited our ranch to check on my mother, he brought his entire family—his wife, mother, father, and the kids. To them, it was like a Sunday outing to visit our place. Not this day.

After Dad called him, Dr. Morris ordered an ambulance to come and take Mom to the Queen of Angels Hospital in downtown LA, about 30 miles away. I knew this had to be serious, because Mom always refused a trip to any hospital. She had collapsible veins and was sorely frightened of needles.

Dad turned and walked out of my home, to be with his wife while they waited for the ambulance to arrive.

And I just stood there some more.

Finally, I gathered up my two babies. Vicki was almost three years old and Ric was about 19 months (15 months apart). By the time I got up the driveway, the ambulance attendants were bringing my mother out of the house on a gurney, rolling her into the wide rear door of the ambulance. In those days, ambulances and hearses looked too similar.

I made it up to that wide, open, rear door, a baby in each arm. My mother was in a semi-sitting position on the stretcher. I called to her, looking in at her, so frail and weak. She raised her hand and almost waved. And I waved back, silently. I did not know that that was to be our last glance ever, my last moment to see her alive.

The ambulance door closed, the ambulance pulled out of the drive, and Dad followed. I don't recall much of what I did or how I reacted except that I remember thinking that my mother was most likely gone.

Mom's wish came to pass. She had often remarked in the preceding months, "I don't know why God doesn't take me home; I'm so ready." She never wanted to go to a hospital. And she never did. She was never admitted to Queen of Angels as she passed away just as Dad arrived at that ambulance back door again. If anyone ever died with grace, my mother was that one.

* * *

And we missed her. Without showing it.

I had already decorated the Christmas tree at my mother and Dad's because that's where we had all planned to be on Christmas morning. That way she could see the grandkids open the toys that she had me buy for them. There were four little ones then. My brother, Ray, and sister-in-law, Joyce, had Debbie (age 4) and Vern (age 2); and I had our two. At that time, we had most family get-togethers at Mom and Dad's home because Mom was homebound. It was the routine. But now Mom was gone!

Frankly, I don't recall how I felt; I do know that we all went through that week with no expressed emotion. We had to "be strong" for the children. In other words, we pretended (as I would call it now) that nothing had changed.

"Grandma is in Heaven, where she was so ready to be."

Since we had reasoned to hold the funeral after Christmas Day, it was a long week. It seemed too "cold" to bury her before Christmas.

We all went through the motions, as we ought to, of preparing for Christmas morning and dinner right there in Mom and Dad's house, as if she was still there.

I continued with all the preparations; and Dad set about, by himself to my knowledge, taking care of all the arrangements for a funeral on the 26th. Our family were personal friends with the mortician from our church, and Mom was taken to the Coon mortuary. I guess we felt that Billy Coon would help Dad with all that needed to be done. My poor father must have felt so alone; and yet, I don't think that a one of us knew how to express needs or much of anything.

"On with the business of living," is how we must have each been thinking.

Our mother was so loved and respected. It was a huge service in the big, old, red brick church (The First Brethren) in Long Beach, the 5th and Cherry Church, as it was referred to where we were from. This was our old home church. The small mission church had been begun closer to the ranch, where we now lived.

The First Brethren denomination was a branch off the old Quakers. I remember as a small child when some Quaker members would visit and share in our service. They were dressed then as they did regularly in their own community, which to me, as a little kid, had seemed "different."

So, the funeral service was held at the big church. It was full of dark wood paneling, pews, creaky carpeted floors, and stained-glass windows. The basement was as big as the upstairs area.

I remember that as a child I was scared to be alone in such a big, dark place, especially in the basement. Of course, I never would have told anyone how scary it was for me. I always felt that I had to be a grown-up lady. My mother had reminded me often growing up, "Be ladylike." So, I had been.

Unfortunately, in the 1960s, someone set fire to that church and numerous other large, old brick churches in Long Beach. To my knowledge, none of them ever recovered.

All the funerals that I had ever been to were so solemn and cold, or so it seemed to me. And at this funeral it felt the same. We sat in the "family" section, over to the side where people could not see us. How I wanted to work up some tears; I could not.

I had known most of my childhood years that Mom could die any day. I remember her talking about it one day when we were out in the garage doing laundry in our old, ringer-type washer at our first home in Long Beach, Mom and Dad's first home that they purchased—made to order with a rare and coveted fireplace. I was only three or four. While I may have been told about Mom dying once earlier, this time stuck with me. Even to this day, I think that that was far too early in my life to be given that information. Mother's reasoning was for me to know that each day was a blessing for her to still be with us and so that I would be prepared for the day that God would take her. You can never be truly prepared. And, with that knowledge I started to protect myself, building a wall that prevented me from getting too close to her.

Therefore, when "that day" came, my thinking was simply, "After all, I am now 20 years old with two babies. I'm all grown up! And, she got to live long enough to see all four of her grandchildren. What a blessing!"

There was no reception at the church before the long, quiet trip over the hill to the burial. After all, we were to be happy and grateful that she had lived this long.

I can remember riding in the family limousine, black of course, as we went up to Signal Hill—it was fully covered with oil derricks—on Cherry Avenue to the Sunny Side Cemetery in north Long Beach. The old cemetary stood atop the hill, in the midst of those derricks. Mom was to be buried further north, in the new cemetery. I recall looking back and saying, "There are cars as far back as I can see."

Today as I look back, I think, "What a sad day." Yet, no emotion was expressed as we had watched her strength slowly ebb for the several years previous. She had truly been so ready to go "home to be with the Lord."

After the burial, our church folks had a dinner ready for all family and guests who chose to join us at Mom and Dad's home. Many people shared that meal.

* * *

Mom had passed away just four years after I was married. That left me a lost pup with an angry master. Dad also was so lost without Mom to take care of. He had taken such good care of her physically for most of their 30-plus years of marriage. Yet, Mom had been the backbone of our entire family, though often ill.

Dad began to reacquaint with some old friends known in the early days of their marriage in the late 20s and early 30s, before Christ had changed their lives. I felt happy for him, because he had been so loyal and faithful, taking care of our mother. He had had no social life for the past few years. Little did I know where that reacquainting would lead him. Little did I know that the entire year was to be one of reigniting his disease of alcoholism, changing the course of our lives—Dad's especially.

I had absolutely no knowledge of what this disease was!

This all occurred during the latter part of Stonnie's active duty, during which time the Korean War was pretty much at an end. My husband was still away a lot. In fact, he was overseas the summer of 1955 and again the later part of 1956, then discharged in 1957.

At age 21, I was so busy trying to be a good and faithful wife and mother, as mine had been. Life as I had known it was about to change drastically yet again. And in more ways than one.

CHAPTER TEN

Truck-Driving

After Stonnie got out of the Navy, Dad helped him get a job with Richfield Oil (later Arco). Stonnie and I then bought a small truck for him to use for work. Promptly, Stonnie lost the oil job due to stealing (unnecessary items and for no good reason). Next, he started doing odd jobs around town. Then he went to work for the crane company in LA for which his brother Bob worked. That did not last long either. He had no experience in any trade, and his adjustment to life outside the Navy was less than smooth.

During that time, I did my grocery shopping at a little market in the neighborhood, Shorty's Market, so named after the owner. We did not have big supermarkets like now exist, and this store was smaller than most.

Shorty was a funny little man with a clear New York Italian accent. Incredibly friendly, he could usually be found in the meat department, where he always gave the kids each a hot dog or "frank" (then known as "wieners") to eat while I shopped. Yes, right out of the showcase! In those days, hot dogs did not come in packages sold by brand name but were loose items found in a big, stacked mound in the meat showcase and sold by the piece or pound. As was true for many people, I generally bought the same order each time I went to Shorty's. I had heard that Shorty had been in the blackmarket meat business throughout World War II.

One day I bought no meat. As I pushed my basket past the meat counter, Shorty spoke to me.

"Hey, you forgot your meat stop."

"Hello, Shorty. And no, I did not forget, but thank you."

"What do you mean? You always buy meat. Why not today?"

I explained quietly that my husband had lost his job, so I was shopping a bit differently this trip.

"I see," said Shorty kindly. "Sorry to hear that."

I thanked him and continued my shopping.

Minutes later, when I was already in another aisle, up walked Shorty, with a brown paper bag. He placed it quickly in my basket with the words, "Tell Papa that this is on Shorty this time."

I just nodded, speechless.

When we got home I discovered, to my silent thrill, that the large package contained— individually wrapped in white butcher paper—almost everything that I normally bought. Shorty was someone who I would never forget.

A short time later, my dad suggested we buy a cow; we did, I believe with his help. A small black Angus cow, Blackie was due to have a calf, which she could do pastured in our next-door neighbor Zelda's back property.

My proud dad.

One morning, ready for school and heading out of the house, one of us looked back and saw not only Blackie but another black creature. How exciting! Blackie had had her baby. Naturally, we stopped our departure and went to see, amid Vicki and Ric both calling out, "Daddy! Daddy! Blackie had her calf!"

Yes, there she was with her little white-faced black baby. I took a couple of pictures with my old box Kodak camera; then off to school we all went. What a morning that was!

As Blackie was a nurse cow, we bought a couple more calves for her to nurse. Somehow, Stonnie really took to the cattle idea. He was off and running making money by dealing young cattle. His business activities soon outgrew his small pickup. Before we knew it, we bought a bobtail truck from a local produce market. Having had it modified to haul calves, Stonnie began buying and selling them from the dairies. He bought them in our area, in what was known at that time as "Dairy Valley," where calves were plentifully available; then hauled them to calf feeders in the San Joaquin Valley in northern California.

In that valley, from north of Bakersfield all the way to Modesto were lots of cattle feeders, always buying calves to feed. Stonnie suddenly had a true business going, grown by his energy and ability to get to know the dairymen, others involved in calf trading, and pretty much everyone on his route.

Never one to let the dust settle under his feet, to keep from returning with an empty truck he started picking up various hauls. One trip he came back with a bunch of baby goats to sell at auction the next week. Of course, we kept them in our backyard, feeding them with bottles until their departure day. The kids loved that!

Ric had a little lamb, Pinky.

A dream I recall from that time was that he brought home a load of snakes that I was trying to contain in the backyard. It seemed so real, and it might as well have been because I never knew what he would show up with next. When it comes to mind, I still wonder about that dream.

Some auction days during the summer, the kids and I joined my husband as he traveled to and from Hanford, California. One such evening in the year 1959, Cliff and I (Stonnie now insisted on going by his given name; he thought it more "professional-sounding"), after hauling some cattle up to northern California, were traveling down Highway 99, coming in to Bakersfield, California.

We had cleaned out the bobtail two-axle truck and made a bed of fresh straw in the back; covered the area with a large tarp, having first taken the kids down to play in the river; freshened up; and gone to eat before heading back down the highway to our home in Artesia. The kids were likely asleep in the back.

As we crossed the track coming to the northern end of Bakersfield, Cliff suddenly slipped across the bench seat stating, "You drive."

He picked me up and plunked me in the driver's seat.

What?!? Oh, my God! I had never driven anything larger than a pickup; I did not even know whether the transmission of this monstrosity was a 4-speed or 6. The most I had ever done with this truck was to move it in low gear to pull away from the loading shoot while Cliff put the cattle in the corral. I had not even a moment to think about this; and here I was, coming into a town trying to slow down! I knew how to downshift a car or pickup, but I was not at all certain how in this thing. And Cliff was talking to me as though I just ought to know. I didn't even have time to be mad because I was so scared.

Obviously, because I am here now writing about the experience, I made it through town and down "The Grapevine" as the stretch of road home was called. Still, I do not remember how I got my kids home safely that night.

In those days, no Class 1 license was required to drive a two-axle. Since I got us home, Cliff now considered me a full-fledged truck driver.

Soon after this time, my kids entered school. Cliff got a job as a cattle salesman at a new stockyard in Artesia. Prior to that, the only stockyard in LA County had been in Los Angeles. As I was now his truck driver, he set it up for me to pick up starter calves from calf-feeding ranches and haul them to the sales yard.

Cliff had also "handled" things on the kid side of my life. In chatting with our neighbor lady, Inez, he had learned that she would be available to watch the kids if needed while I worked. Vicki and Ric were just in kindergarten and first grade. Cliff assured me that this was not something that I would be doing every day, just on sale days. Most of the time, I could take the children to school and be home to pick them up. Later in the year, during vacation, they rode with me if they wanted to and stayed with Inez otherwise.

Of course, as time went on, Cliff set up more and more times for me to bring cattle in. He was obviously charging less than the big cattle-hauling companies, which resulted in me growing busier by the day. As the bookkeeper in my "free time," I did not set prices. That was Cliff too. One thing I can say about that husband is that he had the gift of seeing opportunity when it arose. His mind ran faster than I could keep up. Still, the other trucking companies soon decided that "this truck-driving gal" was taking too much of their business. They began a petition against me!

The stockyard management let Cliff know that I needed to put an end to my hauling; not a business for women, they said. We were making some nice extra money, which I liked; however, I really wanted to be a homemaker, so I did not mind stopping hauling at all. The stay-at-home dream was not going to become a reality for me then.

Forty-plus years later a good friend who worked in the mental health field said (referring to Cliff), "From what you and Vicki tell me about him, it sounds like he struggled with attention-deficit/hyperactivity disorder (ADHD) or some form of mental illness." That explained to me why Cliff had been in special education class for a couple of years as a little boy. And how had that helped? Cliff had also told me that the teacher sat in the front of the class on her desk, facing the students, with her feet on the first desk, legs open, no underwear . . . As he was the one most often in trouble, she sat him right up front so that she could watch him. And he? Well, that's what he learned. It certainly was "special education." How could that not have been an issue in that mid-1930 era? Maybe no-one "told."

At any rate, since I could no longer haul cattle, Cliff looked for other opportunities. No eating establishments were in the near vicinity, so employees who had not brought their own lunch were traveling a mile or more away to pick up something to eat. Soon, I heard him saying that we should be providing lunch and snacks for employees and customers on the property.

His thinking was that we had a neighbor to watch the kids, so "Why don't we buy a brand-new catering truck for you to run?" These rolling food trucks were a new concept in those days.

Well, I liked contributing to making money; and all I would have to do was be out there for all the customers and workers, with food available. Did not sound too bad! Except for the parts that I was not thinking about—like how I would have to be out early each morning to load the truck with fresh food, unload every afternoon, count my money and do the bookwork, do the ordering for the next day, and then cook dinner for our family.

As time went on, I was doing pretty well. Cliff started setting me up for horse stables where riders practiced riding, roping, jumping, and other events. They definitely needed a food truck. And so did other venues and events, as many as Cliff could find and sell to. Soon, I was running the food truck every day of the week. When the kids were not in school, they joined me.

Inez, our babysitting neighbor, had a sister who was a seasonal visitor. She offered to be with the kids and do my laundry as well as light cleaning. Actually, I was doing quite well in that role. Looking back, I can see how God had opened a door for me to go on my own; I just did not see it at the time. It is said that our hindsight is better than our foresight. True! Back then I was just thinking, "Hey, I am really making money with this!"

And life was speeding along so fast for me! Some Saturdays and Sundays serving lunch at Gymkhana events at the stables I found that I needed to return to the supply warehouse and re-stock the truck because I was already running out. I had picked up some big corporations' lunch business during the weekdays! My mistake was in not knowing that I ought not to have accepted any "truck-driving idea" in the first place.

CHAPTER ELEVEN

The Beginning of Verda Cattle Company

Cliff managed to get himself fired from the stockyard job when he had his own opinions and clearly claimed that his were better than the boss'; or maybe he simply indicated that he could do a better job than Mr. Barker could. In any case, he seemed only slightly bothered to have been fired again. He was already working on another deal with one of the clients.

The man was a wealthy contact at the stockyards, and one with whom Cliff had already been discussing a business venture. This was to be a partnership, Cliff running and managing a cattle operation on one of the gentleman's ranches in what is known as Canyon Country. The man's name was Chub; he owned a large rubbish business, among many others.

Vicki and Ric.

Waiting for the bus (home in background).

Chub had previously shut down this ranch. Back in the 40s, maybe even into the 50s, when the trash company had separate garbage trucks for wet goods and people kept separate wet pails to put out that garbage along with the regular trash barrels, the ranch had been a hog operation, cooking the bacteria out of the trash before feeding it to the hogs. In fact, the garbage disposal that we got in the mid 1950s was a novelty at the time. But it's not solely because of the increased of garbage disposals, the departure of the wet pails, or a lack of hogs that the ranch was eventually closed down.

The ranch had been sitting for years because Chub and his brother had back then bought a nice little home for next to nothing in Downey and moved it up to the ranch property to use as their own. His brother was running a crane in relation to the move when it hit a power line, electrocuting him. He did not survive.

The ranchstyle house was ready to live in, except for requiring cleaning and painting inside, having sat empty so long. Chub, a giant of a man, had a large speaking voice, except for the day that he met us there to show us the place. The very act of being there was obviously emotionally difficult for him. This gave me an early glimpse that despite his bold exterior, he was really all heart.

Chub had an old verbal contract with the Knudsen Creamery in LA, which would allow Cliff and me to use their return (past shelf life) and excess dairy products to feed young calves and cattle. Sounded to Cliff like a money maker. This meant that we were to sell the catering truck, rent our current home to the church next door as parsonage for their pastor, and move out to Chub's old out-of-the-way place. The isolated ranchhouse sat on a hill to one side, placed between grandiose mountains on either side of that large multi-acre property. Steps toward our move began immediately, with cleaning at the level of scrubbing, then painting, around the clock. It was November, 1963.

New knowledge for me since my divorce, so not noted then: abusive people love to isolate their families.

As we nonstop readied our new home, up on the hill, with its view of the entire canyon, the news blasted a shocker: President Kennedy had been shot in Texas. So sad, this news made my job feel all the heavier; however, there was no stopping Cliff when he was doing anything. Cliff never started a job and quit before it was done. So, I made a bed for the kids in one of the large closets. Still, I think that we did go home that day. It seems that I recall hearing the news on the truck radio several times throughout our drive home.

Over the course of the next week, after several more long work days at the ranch, we were ready to begin the moving process. The ranch was about 80 miles from our home in Artesia. We loaded the furniture and took off.

When we first moved up there, it seemed that life was going to improve. I loved the house, and I found that I really liked living out in the country. As no cattle were on the grounds yet, it was pretty quiet. Peaceful, even. Little did I know how tough life was about to get!

Chub had a lot of people working for him in many places. One day he moved a Mexican man into a small place down by the pens and work area. We learned that he had been working for Chub for a long time at one of Chub's other properties. Lupe was his name and he was there to help us.

One of Chub's go-to guys, he could work like a horse and was a great man. He loved the kids and me and was so protective! He had a family down in Guadalajara, Mexico; and all his money— except for that for the tortillas, pork chops, jalapenos, and Pepsi Cola that he bought weekly when I took him to the market—went to them. He told me through his broken English that he returned once a year or so to see them and that he had built a nice home for them there.

Our kids were now 9 and 10 years old. I was driving a rickety, old tank truck to LA, about 50 miles away, to pick up milk from the creameries and haul it up to the ranch to feed calves. As there were plenty of rattlesnakes in those hills, I did not want the kids walking to their bus stop, about a ½ mile away. Cliff bought an old car for $5 at auction so that the kids could drive themselves to the mailbox to catch the school bus on days that I was not home in the morning.

During our first summer there the kids and I went to help with the cattle as the trucks came in to unload them in the working pens. Lupe, the kids, and Cliff and I "worked" the cattle before they headed into the feeding pens. This meant we did vaccinations, dehorning, castrations, and any other necessary care prior to their feeding and growing process. Later, we hired one other helper, with a valid drivers' license. That was a big help.

It was hot, dusty, and dirty up there in the high desert. I would take a cooler to work there, with beer for Cliff and sodas for the rest of us. When we took our much-needed break, I would open the beer for Cliff, take a sip, and pass out the sodas. Suddenly, beer tasted good to me. I began taking a beer for me too! In the past, I had tried many alcoholic drinks as it seemed important to Cliff for me to join him in that; but I just could not seem to stomach them. In those times, he would accuse me of thinking that I was "too good" for him and his friends.

Here I was now though, beginning a drinking journey that was to last many years. At the time, the beers I drank kind of took the edge off and helped me tolerate both Cliff's rage and the life we were living. This is so sad, because my kids paid the price.

Cliff had met another rancher down the road who offered him yet another "opportunity." Harry had verbal contracts with most of the large, bread-producing bakeries in LA for feed for his cattle. He had more supply than he could feed out and needed someone to take the excess and do something with it. As we were buying a lot of grain at that time, this bakery bread could be ground and mixed in, thereby decreasing those feed dollars out. All we had to do was remove the packaging. Harry had an old grinder and an auger truck, so we could grind the bread and combine it with the feed to fatten the cattle. Chub felt that it could work for us. We headed into this venture.

Questions, though. Who is going to do this job? Drive the rickety truck with the roll-off container to get it filled at the bakeries? My family, of course; along with Cliff's younger brother, Eddie, and a close friend, Bill, temporarily laid off from Lockheed.

The kids were by then almost in junior high and instructed to come straight home so that "we" could grind bread. That old grinder gave me nightmares. I was so afraid that one of my kids would get a hand in that grinder; no protection existed to avoid that possibility. Vicki and Ric took turns driving the tractor with the front loader to keep loading the grinder, which had a conveyor belt that fed the ground material into the feed truck with the auger. When it came time for feeding, the auger truck driven slowly down the row of troughs augered out the feed. Flour and crumbs caked us white, to the point that we had to remove our clothes outside before going in the house to shower. It makes me itch to write about it!

Cliff's attitude was, "No big deal, just another drop in the financial bucket."

My thinking ran, "When are my kids going to be able to be kids?"

The beef market started decreasing in 1964, and we were feeding all these cattle to become beef. We then had several hundred head, as cattle are counted. The United States was then importing beef from Australia and Argentina, so we began losing money. Chub, bless his heart, says, "Not to worry. I own a packing house near Ventura." So, we began shipping fat cattle to be killed, re-opened the adjoining meat market, and hired more help.

At the time I was working once a week with Chub's bookkeeper, Alice, down in South Gate. We were losing dollars by the day, no matter what; and each time I worked with Alice I felt the pain of it more keenly. One day, I could not keep it together any longer. I walked into Chub's private office, another rickety building, burst out sobbing, and admitted, "We have lost over $200,000 dollars!"

Chub, as I have referenced, was a big German man. He sat there at his extra big desk grinning kindly and telling me not to worry, that everything was going to be okay. I believed him. And I loved him. He had a true lady as a wife and at least seven kids, all of which he provided greatly for and all of whom he was so proud. Nothing like what we had at home.

The following summer, 1965, I was standing at the kitchen sink and started hemorrhaging, blood gushing out of me and pooling on the floor. I had no idea what was happening, and my doctor was down in Artesia. I went to see him, and he gave me a medication which stopped the hemorrhaging but made me very sick at my stomach. I was to stay in bed and keep taking the med. Repeatedly, as it neared time for the next pill, I would start feeling better; however, the bleeding also returned.

My poor little girl was doing her best to fill my shoes in every way; and unbeknownst to me, her own father was being inappropriate with her. One day she slipped a note in my bed while I was sleeping that said, "I love you, Momma, and I miss you." I was so sick that I had no idea what was going on.

After a week or so, I don't remember exactly, Chub showed up at the ranch and asked where I was. Cliff told him that I was in bed, still sick. Chub went home and told his wife what had been going on; she called her doctor, then her doctor called me. He said, "I want to see you at Saint Francis Hospital ASAP." That hospital was in Lynwood, where Cliff's mom lived, maybe 60 miles away.

Cliff was in LA with a truck, so I drove down with the kids and dropped them at his mom's before taking myself to the hospital.

Admitted, blood was drawn; and the doctor ordered a transfusion. He came into my room. "I cannot believe how low your blood is, yet you are so tan and still have so much color."

He did a dilation and curettage (D&C) once I had enough blood. The problem was a polyp in my cervix. I was not going to be driving any time soon.

While I was in the hospital, at some point—because we now had our pickup at the hospital and the kids at his mom's—Cliff picked up Vicki, told her that she was going to drive the pickup at the hospital home, and that he would follow her in his truck. She was not yet 13 years old and she drove all the way back to the ranch! She told me later that she was so scared, driving all that way on the freeway; but she did not tell me then about her dad's behavior with her. Of course, he had told her not to. It is difficult to recall all the details, but the feelings remain strong. Vicki's memory about that time in her life is foggy also.

Since the money was no longer in the beef cattle, Cliff conjured up a new "opportunity." We would now sell the milk and bread products to other ranches feeding calves and hogs. Cliff talked to Chub, who agreed that we could clear the ranch of cattle, selling all the beef at the meat market.

Chub had met and hired a Romanian man in the Ventura area who had owned a packing house and meat business in Romania before the Communist Party put him out of business. This man was working with us in the meat market, so he and Chub eventually worked out something for him to start a kosher killing house. Cruel. I am glad that I had nothing to do with that one. I am sure that kosher houses have had to deal with animal cruelty allegations since then.

We would create a new business, with the creameries and the bakeries.

CHAPTER TWELVE

Overwhelmed

In the midst of our dirty, hot, grinding, cattle-feeding days, I somehow enrolled at Lapin Brothers School of Beauty in Reseda, California, down in the San Fernando Valley. The girls and guys who enrolled right out of high school completed in about 10 months. I had 1,600 hours to complete, and I think that it took me a little over a year. I did pass my State Board of Cosmetology test with flying colors. I remember thinking, "Hey, I am not as dumb as I have grown to believe!" That helped some.

Something else proved to me that I had ability, though I could scarcely comprehend it. One day during beauty school I was kept after class, along with several others. We were told that from that time on we would be along the stylists' wall, as stylists, versus in the center with the other students. Student equaled lower pricing; stylist equaled higher pricing. Me, a stylist? I did not feel like one; and I could hardly believe that I was among those who were actually stylists. At the time, Vidal Sassoon was a big name, and he had follower stylists who took outrageous hair risks. That was not me. I did, however style a great bouffant each time, prior to graduating.

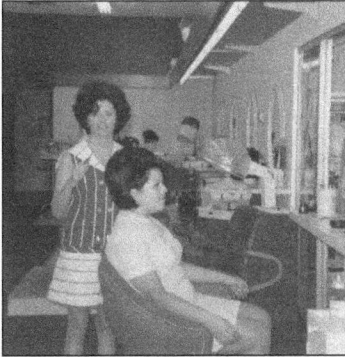
Stylin'!

Reception desk.

I started working for a small beauty shop, Clip and Curl, near where we lived; and I began building a nice clientele, still keeping books for the two businesses and only driving on occasion. Still helping with the grinding and feeding, and continuing nightmares related to my kids running that damned grinder.

With the hair styling, I could pretty much set up my schedule to just fit everything in. Maybe I could somehow make and save enough for my kids and I to branch out on our own. I was certainly not thinking about adding anything into my life; however, Cliff was. He discovered a similar small shop around the corner, for sale. His take was, "It's a better location; and if you're the owner, you collect a percentage of the other girls' work plus 100 percent of your own."

Well, that made perfect sense to Cliff, whose thinking was all "Make money!"

My thinking had been about how to get my kids and move on. Still, making money made me think, too. Soon, I was the owner of a shop with three other chairs; and we were earning more money. Writing about how easily I could be manipulated by my own husband, to the detriment of my own children, is not easy.

Not only did Cliff have a gift of manipulation, he was also a good delegator. He could shuffle all of us like a dealer in a poker room; keep us doing the work so that he could be out drumming up new opportunities. Soon, he was negotiating with the owner of a new strip mall, to open a grand salon of eight chairs or more.

It was grand, largest in the entire Canyon Country. I still had the small ones around the corner with the three girls. Verda's Beauté Boutique opened in August 1968. The first actual salon in the area, it immediately drew a good clientele. I had one of the girls, Margo, run the little shop. I had acquired her services with the purchase of it. I went to work in the new place along with Irma, Katy, Martha, Debbie, Jeannie, and Edith.

Next to the salon on the south side was a dental office and on the north side was a strictly Italian deli. Next door to the deli was a paint store. Soon after we opened, the week before Thanksgiving, we were so busy (related to advertising) that we were booked through New Years with bouffants. Unbeknownst to us, the Italian couple at the deli were not getting along. Very early on Thanksgiving morning they had a big fight, which we later learned was the reason for the wife blowing up the store. The firefighters were so busy keeping the fire away from the paint store so that no chemicals contributed to further explosions that my place suffered greatly. That gave me a supposedly good reason to tie one on that day, not drinking to drunk, but definitely to the place of not caring as much.

Vicki modeling.

Vicki modeling.

Popular coordinates.

Thanks to having the small salon around the corner, we were able to move most of our bookings there. The owner of the shop next to that salon, proprietor of a small dress shop, offered space for my dryers, hoping to garner more business for herself. Together, we all succeeded.

The following February, however, a huge, flooding storm that moved in every direction and even closed down schools claimed the bar at the end of that mall when it fell into the wash. Initially, the dress shop owner moved several items to my salon for display and sale, but eventually that entire building was condemned. The dress shop owner closed shop for good.

Through that Cliff lost no time developing a new idea and getting me to do the ongoing work of it. Back in our large salon, we added claim to the former deli and became dress shop owners! Antique displays were all the rage; and I was good at obtaining them, at whatever sale we might find, in town or out. During that time, we still managed to take overnight trips up the coast, in the Mora Bay area, hitting all the "junk" stores open. Cliff specialized in obtaining dress racks; checkout counters; and unique, three-way dressing room mirrors. Once our additional venture was all set up, Cliff backed away again; and I overlooked the store dealings, not that I had the time.

We often stayed in Los Angeles at the Biltmore. There, on a certain floor, we could attend the vendor show, where each room boasted a different piece of apparel or accessory. Most were owned by New Yorkers, each vying for their "old friends'" attention, and big buying of each style, by size multiples. This exhausted me more than any other part of owning a dress shop. Before braving those money-hungry and inexhaustible darlings,

I always stopped to enjoy a get-me-through-this drink at the classy, carved wood bar downstairs. Ambiance was a draw for my drinking.

One repeat event that I really DID enjoy from owning a dress shop combined with a salon was the fashion show that we hosted once every season or so. This event was inspired by Jeannine, a pretty lady who had improved her bony physique and confidence with a minor boob job. Cliff handled having the display pedestal made and painted, I provided coffee and sweets, and Jeannine ran the event. A combination of girls from the salon and some of our hair clients served as everything from model to coffee server, and our sales certainly went up related to those afternoons.

During the time of our grand salon transaction, Cliff had found a partially built home up in Acton, California. On 26 acres, it had three bedrooms and one and a half baths and was affordable. To purchase that property, we necessarily sold the rental, our original home in Artesia, to the church, which made both them and us happy. We paid $24,000 for our new home and property. The deal was written up so that the owner/seller carried the papers, and we paid it off in two years.

The outside and the roof were finished. Cliff's older brother Russ, a tile setter and handy, was not working at the time, which worked out for us; he could finish the interior. Cliff, of course, was not the hands-on kind of working guy, rather a person who liked being in control.

Interior, as purchased.

First snow- rear.

First snow- road to the house.

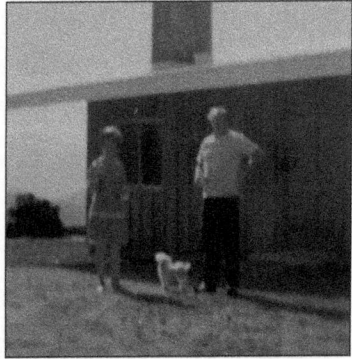

Outside, as purchased.

I began doing the shopping with Russ for all needed materials. Russ and Cliff both had pickup trucks, so Russ helped haul things to the house. I ordered custom, solid birch unfinished cabinets for the kitchen. Then, after dinner and any other time that I could find, I worked on the finishing, stain, and polyurethane—four coats—doing the rubbing with fine steel wool after each coat. They were really pretty! That was something that I really enjoyed doing, putting my general shop education into practice.

Still, I was feeling so overwhelmed with everything in my life. I hired a bookkeeping service to help me keep all the separate accounts. The bookkeeper, Gary, suggested that, because we had so many more endeavors than just cattle, we create a new name: Verda Cattle Enterprise. By then we had a payroll to do. I had three different checkbooks; Gary had me put the invoices and receipts of each business in separate manila envelopes. Each month, he journalized them. I did the banking and check writing, coding each check stub for him to enter in the journals. Gary told me kindly that he thought I was a bit on overload and that I needed to stand up for myself. While I agreed with him, I could not see how to change anything. To me, it was like trying to jump from a fast-moving merry-go-round—how and when do I jump?

In the midst of it all, we still had fun! We threw parties, usually on Sundays. I did the planning, made the arrangements, and did all the cooking. Added to that craziness, Cliff and our good friend, Bill, bought a boat! This was a 28-foot, wooden-hull cruise yacht, all old teak wood. For us, it was a BIG boat about which Cliff felt confident connected to his and Bill's combined boating experience in the Navy. Large enough for the four adults to sleep below, our combined couples' seven kids and any of their visiting friends easily put out sleeping bags and pads and slept above on deck, which could be enclosed by a form of zip-down tarps. Often, these weekend jaunts meant trips to Catalina Island, sometimes with the kids and others not. The boat and its attached motorized dinghy were moored in Redondo. The kids, Ric especially, enjoyed puttering around throughout the marina in the dinghy, which held three. As a family and couple we had to enjoy our toys often! For me that meant more shopping, more traveling, more wardrobe considerations, more stress, more exhaustion, and... MORE DRINKING. To help get everything done, I paid Vicki to do laundry and clean house. Besides that, upkeep on the boat was non-stop. As the men did that part, Cliff soon tired of the boat. He was off to other busy endeavors.

The boat.

The 1972 earthquake, the epicenter of which was in Sylmar, California, was the beginning of the end of the salon. Its shaking destroyed all the glass containers filled with tints, color, and dyes. My plate glass window shattered, shredding the second set of beautiful new drapes; the stations, however, were pretty much intact, so we kept working.

Inside, though, I was done, though we did rebuild and begin again. As always I asked God to help me. The problem was that I had never gotten out of His way while I pushed through on my own; and I rarely did even for years after that, though I also never forsook my daily devotional time.

One day, later that year, I finally turned to God during one of my constantly pleading daily devotionals and said, "Okay, God; I think that You don't want me in this business." Shortly after that, a buyer seemed to appear out of nowhere. We sold. As an afternote, even more than a decade later, when I happened by again, it was still Verda's Beauté Boutique!

Cliff had insight and impetus to put in initial sweat equity, then, once whatever it was was set up, he backed away from any actual ongoing physical involvement and headed to the next idea. I learned years later that this is what co-dependent, aggressive people do. Life was simply going too fast then. That makes writing about it now difficult.

On the good side of that "rolling with an idea," Cliff had the God-given gift to see an opportunity. Most times, over dinner and drinks in a restaurant his brain spinning, he would suddenly say, "Write this down!" and I did. That meant Verda works magic with figures, sometimes writing on a napkin, at high rates of Cliff's fast-thinking speech.

Admittedly, any given idea sounded great in the relaxed present moment, as long as the bottom line showed profit. My thinking was that I needed to climb higher on the ladder to get to that "happy-ever-after."

It was implementing that wore me out. Every new project took more money and more manpower; and I only had so much steam to rob Peter to pay Paul—completing payroll and billing, determining which bill to pay on which day, and running to the mailbox hoping that something was coming in from somewhere. I repeatedly reminded Cliff, Vicki, and the other truckers to collect from our customers. With Cliff, this often resulted in shouting matches with the very customers he had recently schmoozed. This drove me to more drinking and crying and more drinking. A lot of drama, but I kept living in the middle of it, trying to forget how busy and exhausted I was.

Vicki and I working.

Cliff and Verda at work.

Cliff found a property for sale in downtown LA, adjoining the Santa Monica freeway. We had already been renting from the City of LA a large plot under the freeway to work the creamery and bakery products and park our trucks and trailers. There, we had a small travel trailer that we used as an office and sometimes slept in after a long day, rather than driving the 75 miles home. So, by the time that Cliff found that property, I had already paid off the 26 acres where we had finished the house.

That's when I walked into our bank, where I had a good relationship with Charles Weeks, the president, and said, "Charlie, I need a loan."

He suggested that I use as collateral our clear-title property in Acton. We did it and were thereby able to swing a deal with the owner-seller. The nearest cross streets were Alameda and Olympic, downtown.

After we bought that property, life did not slow down. So many events happened. We added to our vehicle inventory as the business expanded, with Cliff buying trucks and equipment faster than I could figure out how to pay. We both loved a great deal! We had a varying payroll with as many as 30 employees, and a huge gas war broke out. Vicki rented an apartment with one of our female employees and moved on in her life, including pregnancy. Ric enlisted in the Navy. While our sexual relations never dwindled, Cliff and I were emotionally disconnected and nothing more than business partners.

And then, because of the gas war, we rented an apartment closer to our business. Cliff was cheating at the time. In every way. I was totally broken inside. I was drinking every day. I was misbehaving. And I was cheating, too. Times would change, but not before I experienced much more personal turmoil.

Three decades later, 20 years sober, single, and a realtor working as a travel notary, I drove by out of curiosity to see what had become of that former business property of ours. It was a gentleman's club; in other words, a strip club. Interesting. I'm certain that Cliff would have liked that progression.

CHAPTER THIRTEEN

My Promiscuous Years

Having recently filed for divorce and drinking even more, I was not operating in my own true character. I had driven to Big Bear, California, upon invitation of my friend, quite a guy. He was a man for whom I had begun doing bookkeeping in his home office. This man, an engaged man way younger than me, was also the guy with whom I was having an affair. When he one day mentioned a fine restaurant near his construction job in Big Bear, I said that it sounded great.

My cheating lover said, "Why not join us? It'll be me, my buddy, and my fiancée."

Booking a room in the same motel where they were staying, I went. At dinner, his buddy, a married man, got friendly. And after dinner, he came to my room and we continued "the conversation." I had no business being with any of those people at that time. Behaving promiscuously, I was chasing after happiness in all the wrong ways.

On the way home from Big Bear, at a honky-tonk bar, I met a younger guy, Doug, and danced the night away. This was in a tiny town in California: Little Rock, just outside of Palmdale. I had stopped there to spend the night.

I must have given Doug my number because he called, and I began dating him. He was just a few years older than my own two kids and we had a lot of fun together! We often went to his brother and sister-in-law's home. He and his brother liked to play ping pong and were both quite good. His sister-in-law, Judy, worked for the California Department of Employment. I liked our time there, and I liked her.

During the course of our visits, I mentioned needing a part-time job as my daughter Vicki and I had both quit working for the then incorporated Verda Cattle Company. Vicki, then recently married, had gotten a job driving a school bus with William S. Hart School District in Newhall and no longer needed me to care for her daughter, Amber.

Always pretty good at doing repair jobs around the house, one day I was up on my roof in my bikini fixing the makeshift, solar-inspired, crisscross, black hosing system which warmed our pool when I heard the phone ringing. Mind you, this was before anyone had a cell phone. I descended the roof to answer the phone.

It was Judy. She was bubbling over with excitement about an available job that had just come across her desk.

"Verda," she gushed, "you have to go talk to this lady; her name is Pat. This is right up your alley, and you can choose the hours and days that you want to work!"

I thanked her, showered, and drove over to Pat's office. Less than an hour into our conversation, I had a new job! I would be doing payroll, journaling, and balancing the company checking account. It was all that I did for my own company, and all that I loved doing.

Payroll consisted of about 100 people each week. Six women employees worked there; the rest were men. A newly single woman's dream as most of the gentlemen were also single, this made for a fun job for me! I must say that it was an especially attractive time in my life, and I got a lot of attention from many of these guys as they began stopping by my desk—to the point that Pat, also single, had to remind them, "Verda's got work to do! You need to get back to yours!"

This time reinforced awareness of my personal attractiveness, as opposed to what I had been listening to for the past twenty-five years.

The bookkeeping system was called "pegboard accounting" and involved two carbon pages. Before computers, this consisted of a check, a duplicate, and the journal page. A carbon was placed between each. To this day, my right hand is a bit messed up from writing all those checks by hand through the carbons each week. It did keep me from separate journal entries for each, however!

Located in Soledad Canyon, the job itself was at an exotic animal compound. The animals were being used in the motion picture business. This business includes some unique people who live quite interesting lives. Most of them each aspire to be "THE" star. Making a movie was not uncommon in Canyon Country, in the small community of Acton.

The compound included some old buildings used as offices, makeup room and editing room, and a welding shop. The latter was next to our office. Also present were some older travel trailers in which some of the groundsworkers lived. A movie set out in the middle of the property was built much like a jungle scene. Lions, tigers, panthers, an elephant, and even some zebras resided there—to mention some of the animals.

Just driving up the canyon road, one would not have guessed that all that was down there along the riverbed, where a small stream ran through the canyon.

One day I was working at my desk with my door open to the outside. My office was small, about nine feet square containing many filing cabinets. Stacked boxes lined the walls, occupying nearly a third of the room. Likely, this room had been a storage room before my desk and chair were placed in it and it became an office. Despite the lack of space, my office was also the place where new baby animals born on the property were housed for a few days for safety and nurturing while those in charge determined next placements. This day I was the only creature present in my work quarters. It was summer, and the swamp cooler was on in the other room. With the door open, the cool air was drawn into my office space.

I heard a bit of commotion going on outside, not unusual. Suddenly, a large female tiger stood in my doorway. My boss, Pat, in the next office heard me as I spoke calmly, "Pat, a tiger is coming through the doorway." I remained almost motionless.

"Stay still, and go under your desk if you need to," she replied. I did not move. I just sat there, like a statue. The tiger was huge, about 600 pounds I later learned. She glided effortlessly through my space, practically rubbing against the corner of my desk to pass; then padded through Pat's, past two other desks, and directly through the open outside door.

I quickly rose and closed my outside door so that she would not make the same round again. What a beautiful animal! And, I lived to talk about the experience!

Another day, I came to work to learn that a young jaguar cub, Henry, was present. As a newborn, he was being cared for in my office! I was told by the handlers that mothers will not care for their cubs in captivity, so the cubs are necessarily taken away. Having Henry in my office was fun! I have kept several pictures taken with Henry's slightly older sister, Patricia.

Later, a pair of lion cubs was born on the ranch, causing excitement for all! They too, were brought to my office for safekeeping and care. This was wonderful! Within a few days, however, Tippi, Noel's wife and star of the show (known to many today from Alfred Hitchcock's *The Birds*), took them into her home, also on the property, to care for them. Again, I was told that if they had been left with their mother, she would have harmed them. I still don't know if that is factual.

Baby Henry.

Baby ostrich, my office.

At times, I needed to go up to Tippi's house to eat our company-provided lunches. The cubs, then a few months old, played like domestic kittens. They hid behind the sofa, jumped out at my legs, and tried to tackle me. They had already clawed her furniture to shreds, just sharpening their claws on armchairs and such. Cute when young, as they grew older they actually could successfully tackle an adult. Still, Tippi loved those amazing animals as though they were her own children.

Personally, I have always loved animals; however, I now know the great difference between the domestic and the exotic.

I loved that job. It was truly fun! Even when I took a vacation, I was eager to get back to my workplace. I liked doing books for someone else, and not being the one tasked with worrying about the bank balance. I also thoroughly enjoyed getting attention from all those guys. Memories from those years are so good.

One vacation that Doug and I took during that time was to Puerto Vallarta and Mazatlan, Mexico. This included a fishing trip during which Doug caught a marlin. It hurt my heart to see the men beating that and the other fish to knock them out before they pulled them into the boat due to big "swords" on these fish. They caught three that trip. I would have liked to see the crewmen cut them loose, but the guys that caught them wanted to mount them as trophies. One of the fish was a large mahi mahi. Those marvelous creatures come up out of the water with the most vivid colors anyone could ever imagine. It physically hurt me to see them being killed. That was a big difference between Doug and myself.

Fishing trip with Doug.

Another difference between Doug and me was that I was eager to get back to work while Doug was not. I really loved the work that I was doing, the magnificent animals and their sounds, and the overall atmosphere. Another major reason for looking forward to returning was the attention from my male co-workers. And that did not really fit in with keeping Doug around. In fact, Doug told me that one of those guys, Chris, was someone I needed to avoid. Too late! Chris, a hot cutie was a man to whom I gave many gifts, especially clothing, which fulfilled my fantasies of who I wanted him to be. And, of course, based on who I was at that time, I gave him numerous other attentions. This was easy because I had never developed a love for Doug. I had cared for him, but I had not had the love and commitment needed for a long-term partner. Operating in self-seeking sensuality more than in love, I may have helped to define "promiscuity" in those years. And that was not a goal I set out with in life.

One who was not promiscuous was my son, Ric, discharged from the U.S. Navy, enrolled in medical school, and living in Sacramento on his GI bill. He was also working part time as an (emergency medical technician) EMT for an ambulance company and doing well. Rescuing others, animals and people, was a part of his personality. Despite these good traits, at the time I was concerned about Ric because as far as I knew he had still not dated at the age of 24.

One day, as I learned from him after the fact, a park bench changed all of that.

Walking by, Ric saw a girl crying. He turned around to make sure that she was okay, to learn that she was not. She was probably somewhere between 15 and 16 years of age. Talking to her as he had to so many other strangers, he learned quite a bit; and they both enjoyed the exchange enough to continue it.

I did not know a thing about the relationship until Ric, needed back in LA by Cliff to help his dad, dropped everything he had going in Sacramento and brought the girl with him to Verda Cattle.

One day, meeting for lunch, Ric told me not only about their meeting, but that Karen was a great cook, that she prepared superb lunches for him every day, and that I would really love meeting her. What a surprise! I knew little more about her situation in life until I got an unexpected call from San Francisco, from Karen's Italian grandmother!

Grandma informed me of who she was and asked me if I knew where her runaway granddaughter, Karen, was. She also told me that Karen was prone to running, including having previously taken off with her little sister on a bus from Sacramento to San Francisco. Surprised, I told her that I would check into the situation and get back to her. Hanging up from her I immediately called Ric and told him that Karen had better call her grandmother and let her know where she was and what she was doing. If she did not, I would.

CHAPTER FOURTEEN

Out of the Blue

After working for the motion picture production company for about three years, with those years and two additional before involving no contact from Cliff, he called me out of the blue.

"I've done some life-changing work with a program called EST, in Hollywood. Can you bring the baby (Amber, our granddaughter) on Sunday? I want to take you two horseback riding, Verda." Cliff had been doing some business with one of our old friends on a ranch out in Chino, California. The request itself should have been a red flag to me, but I really wanted to believe him.

With all my heart, I wanted our marriage to get better and last. The big problem was that I was still drinking and therefore not thinking too clearly.

The horseback riding was short-lived, and I have limited memory of the day. I do recall that we went to a nice Italian restaurant in Hollywood, near where he was at that time living with a young girl that he had met at his EST group. Payton, as Cliff boasted, was a call girl, currently out of the country with a client.

No matter. After he wined and dined me that evening, I agreed to see him again. We planned to meet for brunch the next weekend.

That afternoon I arrived and waited over an hour for him to show up. Once there, Cliff explained that he had spent the previous night with Payton's female friend from Africa, Moonah. Of course, he legitimized the event with a detailed story.

After the story (which included that the girls were bi-sexual and they had all three engaged in group sex) and much apology for his tardiness, we had our brunch. I today have no idea why I would have listened, much less stayed. But I was in a different place in my head then.

Lunch was served with "all you can drink champagne." During our visit, Cliff asked me to go and see the great old Tudor home that he and the young Payton were remodeling in Hollywood. That interested me. I liked remodeling, and Cliff knew it. By the time our conversation reached that point, it was late evening. As I lived distant, in the high desert, he convinced me that I should spend the night.

Once again, he had hooked me like a dumb fish. After all the time that I had spent swearing to myself that I was so done with him. All my good sense went out the window with a bottle plus of wine! I can still get angry at myself thinking about my decision-making those years.

As time would have it, the night of visiting Cliff's Tudor home, while I was not at my place, my cat Delilah exited the doggy door, likely looking for me. As she had been surgically de-clawed by her former owner, this was not good.

My home was built on the top of a sloping hill, with an extended deck out back. When I went home the next day I looked everywhere and finally found Delilah under a corner, near the doggy door, dead. Doug's dogs had cornered her and killed her; she had died defenseless.

Yes, you read that right. I had been housing Doug's dogs while he was in transition living in an apartment that did not allow big dogs. I had my own dogs, so his added were no problem. I kept them, and from time to time he and I had contact.

I called Doug immediately and told him that he simply had to come get Maggie and Molly, no matter where they had to go. Everything about my life seemed again in turmoil, a huge contrast from four-plus years of personal peace gained from living alone enjoying the positive feedback of others as well as the passing admiration of young men at work.

I craved security and a happy ever after, not strife and death. And after one night with Cliff, everything seemed headed to hell again. So, what wise action did I take? Not a single one other than having Doug remove his dogs from my property. Chances are that I also chose to have a drink to wash it all away.

And then, over time, Cliff and I got together again. And further, against all my developed sound common sense and despite our previous history, I, with Cliff, bought and moved in to another home on a new hill, in Hacienda Heights California.

But the new-to-us home and passage of time were not enough to have healed anything. We fought off and on, and Cliff often visited Payton in New York. And all of that led to MORE mind-altering drinking, followed by more bad decision-making. The cycle of that drug continued, as it always will.

One morning, still in the first year of that cycle, Doug called me. He told me that he had stopped drinking and that he was getting married that very day. I congratulated him, did not confess my own drinking, and confided that I had never since experienced a sexual climax like those with him. He thanked me, we gave each other best wishes, and I never heard another word from him.

About a year later, Doug's new wife called me to let me know that Doug was no longer with us, but that she wanted to have a visit with me, which we did set up, though I was puzzled about the request. She came, we talked for about half an hour, and then she told me that the night he passed away Doug spoke about me and my sexuality with him. Oddly, she seemed to admire me. I told her that I did not understand why Doug would even mention me. That was because my thinking about myself was so low. I only vaguely understood that Doug had passed away by killing himself through drunken suicide.

The visit ended as Doug's widow complimented me on our lovely home, thanked me for the time, and looked at me as though cementing the reality of my existence and the reality of Doug's absence.

Alcoholism, the great debilitator and killer, had struck again.

Looking back now, I think that I needed the next four years living with Cliff to prove to myself that:

1. I too had a real drinking problem.
2. I really did not want to be living the kind of life that I was living.
3. I no longer wanted to be married to Cliff.

Cliff was not the right person for me. For that reason, I had to choose to let go of the dreams of a lifetime marriage and of keeping the family together. Finally, I reached the place where I was ready to do that. I don't know why it took me so long. I had thought that I was there five years prior, the first time I filed for divorce. So, one would think that I had arrived at a good place.

No.

Unfortunately, I still would not yet let go of one big trouble: the alcohol.

That would take me nearly six more years.

* * *

Finally, one evening after dark in 1983, as I staggered down my street, paranoid and desperate, walking my little dogs, I pleaded with God for help.

"God, I don't want to live like this any more!" I said it, and I meant it.

In December of that same year, I was able to stop smoking. A couple of months later, nearly a week before my birthday, on March 9, 1984, I found my way to an AA meeting. I did not tell Cliff, but he had noticed that I had not had a drink for about a week. He suggested a liter of wine to celebrate my birthday.

I agreed, again proving to myself that I was powerless to stop the drinking on my own. The next day I attended a meeting again. Then I drank a glass of wine daily and then attended a meeting daily, sometimes twice or three times a day. I stopped that pattern on April 23, having reinforced the message of quitting enough. There's more to that month's story, too. But I will simply say now that I was THEN FINALLY able to begin the lifelong process of not drinking any more.

Finally, I could really start living the life that God intended me to live. And though that life has not been without struggles, I am happy to report that I have been continuously living that life ever since; and what a journey it has been.

CHAPTER FIFTEEN

A Look Back

The date was May 18, 1984. Ric and Karen were in California from Arizona as we were all going to Shari and Willie's wedding. Shari's parents, Bill and Caroline, were our best friends; they felt like family.

I had been a member of AA for not quite one month. I don't remember much about the ceremony, but I do recall that the venue was park-like. Afterward, we headed to the reception area, which was lined with long tables.

We had just found a place to sit when servers began placing pitchers of beer and wine on the tables. A large pitcher was placed right in front of me. I began to tremble. I must have had some look on my face because Vicki, sitting next to me suddenly asked, "Mom, what's wrong?"

I replied, "I don't know."

"Let's take a walk," she suggested. I complied. We walked to the restrooms and around that area.

When we came back, the booze was gone, and I felt much better.

I remember little about the rest of that day, with one large exception. I knew that I was going to announce to the family, including Cliff; my daughter; her husband, Steve; our son, Ric; and Ric's wife, Karen while they were in town from Arizona that I needed a divorce. I wanted to do that with all of them together so that no "he said/she said" kind of situation could arise later.

I began the announcement by quoting, in part, the Serenity Prayer. "I am asking God to help me accept the things that I cannot change, which is you, Cliff. You have even told me for years that you are not going to change. I believe you now. And, I am asking God to help me have the courage to change the things that I can change, which is me." I continued, "In order to do this, I need to file for divorce. I won't be going on that trip that we have planned for this week."

Next, we all experienced a moment of tears, after which Cliff left the room. The air remained somewhat heavy.

Our original plan had been to take the RV to a park down south, out of San Diego, that next week. But this was the beginning of the end of our 33-year marriage. I felt so sad. The next day Ric and Karen left for Arizona. The day after that Cliff left, alone, with one of our dogs and the RV. I had made my amends to him in private. I told him that I was sorry that this was hurting all of us, that I had pretended to be happy for too long, and that I had used unhealthy coping skills to make up for it.

Then, home alone, I called a friend of mine in AA, Dan, an attorney. As it was 1984 and the Olympics were to be held in LA, the City had been requesting several changes to our business downtown, to improve appearance and clean up a bit. I had sought counsel for our company from Dan previously. Cliff had talked to him, and Dan had written some letters for us. Here I was now, calling him again, requesting that he handle our divorce.

"I'm sorry, Verda. I cannot do that. It would be a conflict of interest."

I replied, "Okay. If you were getting a divorce, who would you call?"

His reply was not immediate. "Let me get back to you on that, Verda."

By the next week, he had a name for me. I called that attorney, whose office was also in downtown LA, near Dan's.

After our initial conversation, I went there to meet the recommended attorney.

As he greeted me, he commented, "Your name is so familiar."

I found that strange as our name was actually unusual. In fact, I always checked the phone book when we traveled to see if anyone listed had our last name. As it turned out, this was the same attorney who had handled my eldest granddaughter Amber's adoption as Steve's daughter after Vicki and Steve were married! That introduction, looking back on it, was another act of God! I mean, how many attorneys were there in LA? At the time I glossed over it as mere coincidence. No such thing.

In this matter of Cliff and my divorce, we had to talk property. For this, being the bookkeeper in the family, I used a five-column columnar. In Column #1, I made a list of our properties and all assets. In Column #2, I listed the values of everything that we owned. These included the California ranch and the Arizona ranch, along with our many other commercial and residential properties. Business property was entered as were household property, antiques, furniture, and all the rest. So were personal vehicles and RV. All trucks, semi-trailers, and equipment were included. One for him; one for me. And so on. In the fifth column, I again listed all values. In this manner, when the two columns (#3 and #4) are tallied, the bottom line of those columns equals the total of the fifth. Old school accounting.

Once this was completed, I intended for Cliff to choose a column—I was prepared to take the column that he did not choose. The dollar values of each were the same. And they were significant.

My paperwork in hand, I attended my next appointment with the attorney. He mentioned that it was a clever plan, requested that I give him a $700 retainer, and encouraged me to contact Cliff to see if he might visit the attorney to discuss values. Perhaps we could come to some agreement out of court, and at no additional charge.

I told Cliff that I had retained an attorney; if he wanted to retain his own, fine. I added, "However, if you want to choose a column, we can just use the one representative."

Cliff made an appointment with the attorney that I had hired, discussed the columns, and made his choice. We signed an agreement, and it was done. We were divorced in the time that it took the attorney to appear and file. Then came the six-month wait for finalization.

The first time that I had filed, ten years prior, had been such a fiasco. Cliff had said then, "If I wanted a divorce, I could just walk." So, we had both hired attorneys. At the courthouse, Cliff was yelling so loudly at both attorneys that they moved us to a padded room to decrease the noise. I think Cliff had thought that he was going to out-manipulate those two professionals. We walked away that time with two big bills and nothing accomplished.

This second time around, I think that we were both ready to throw in the towel. Simple. Completed without even going to court. DONE! I was FREED!

Yet, I had in my spirit a heavy feeling of grief that I could not understand.

A lady friend at my church lost her husband to cancer as I was divorcing. I felt that while she had a real reason to have a heavy heart, I did not. Then, it slowly dawned on me: This heaviness of mine was because I was also grieving. I was mourning the loss of the dreams of a life-long marriage and the ability to drink alcohol like a lady. I had heard about a grief recovery workshop at the local hospital. I signed up to attend. There, I learned that I simply had to walk through the pain of my loss.

Years later, Cliff called me and wanted a copy of the columnar from our divorce. I could not find it, so I called Dan again to see if he had the attorney's current phone number (the one I had was out of service). Dan informed me that the man was now a judge and gave me his number.

Hard to believe, he remembered me even after almost ten years. He said, "I know that I have it in one of my large piles of files. If you can give me some time, I'm sure that I can find it."

I recalled the wall-to-wall piles and files in his office. I agreed, of course.

A few days later, he called me back. Yes, he had it and was happy to mail it via US post! Unimaginable. This was before personal email and FAX. Another answer to unspoken prayer.

* * *

I have learned so much during my life since my divorce. From my daily Bible reading I have learned that I was so ignorant before!

When I speak of ignorance, I am talking about a lack of awareness and a lack of experience, not a lack of intelligence. It hurts to have to remember and re-live the blind ignorance from which I suffered. I knew that actions and states of being did not feel right; however, the only excuse I have for how naïve I was is simply that I was just a kid trying to know how to be an adult, thinking that I was an adult, but lacking life experience

CHAPTER SIXTEEN

Dreams

During the time that I was seeing a counselor in my early recovery, I was having terrible dreams. He had me write what I could remember of them. Some still stand out so vividly, even from when my children were quite young. Some came true years later. Based on various teachings and my morning Bible reading, I would say that they were "fulfilled."

For example, when Ric was a toddler I had a heart-pounding dream that Cliff got angry (as often), picked Ric up, threw him down on his head, and his head broke. Maybe this was because Cliff often said of Ric, "I'll break his spirit!"

When I told Cliff about the dream, he asked, "What do you think I am, a monster?"

Well, that was a monster of a dream, and I consider it a pre-warning of Ric's then impending mental health diagnosis. Ric was such a cute little boy with so much personality; I think that Cliff was jealous of that.

As it turned out, Cliff did break that spirit and Ric's head was eventually "broken" with mental illness. How sad. And I allowed that to happen, though it hurt my head and caused that and many other bad dreams. I believe that God was speaking to me then; I just could not hear Him yet.

I also had a dream for years about Cliff's elbow pushing in the middle of my spine. Cliff would even wake me some of these nights because I was crying out, "Please, no more!" Interesting that I never had that dream again after our divorce.

CHAPTER SEVENTEEN

My Experience at Ralee

Following my decision to become truly single and change my lifestyle, I spent the first couple years of my sobriety in a narrow space of living: I went to meetings (up to five a day!), went to church, worked at the church, agonized about what I could offer any other job, and wondered about getting a job.

I had never had to go out and present myself to get a "real" job. I did not know how to either. I was over fifty years old and did not know what I had to offer a business outside of one that was my own.

Along with keeping all the records for our own company, and still drinking every day, I had been volunteering for the past year at both my AA center as treasurer, purchaser, and chairperson; and at my church as what they titled the financial secretary. I was trying to please God by doing something to earn His favor as well as the favor of His people.

Along with two other ladies, I counted the offerings every Monday. I made up the bank deposit and went to the bank. Each week I manually entered each regular giver's statement in a 5 by 7 card file. Then, at the end of each quarter, I placed the file box out in the narthex of the church for the members to pick up so that each might see his or her own record of giving. At the end of the year, I tallied them for each giver's tax return.

In the meantime, I attended Alcoholics Anonymous meetings every day.

I had never used a computer. One day I was at the church doing my job when the gal at the upper part of the Financial Committee came in and informed me that the giving program was to be set up on a computer system.

Right away, I said, "I will have to resign because I know nothing about computers."

The next Monday morning the gals (both local businesswomen and both with computer systems for their businesses) and I were doing our counting when one spoke up, "Verda, you can do this!"

The other agreed.

I did not believe that, but did agree, after much persuasion, to try. I realized later that that was God's way of preparing me for a "real" job. Not only that, but this church family, which

I had joined, was teaching me how to walk in the business world. I was then told that I needed a resumé. I had no idea how to prepare one. One of the men on the Finance Committee volunteered to help me. Thank you, God.

Very soon, I began looking for ads in the paper, making visits to employment offices with my resumé in hand, trying with shaking knees to get a job!

One day I was coming home from one of those interviews and was passing a company along the way that my own company had used as a vendor in the past. As I passed it, I found myself slowing and pulling into a parking lot on the other side of the street so that I could turn around and go back. I thought, "I can go in to the familiar place and see if they need help." After all, it would be a start. However, as I looked where I had pulled in, I found myself thinking, "This looks like it would be a good place to work." So, I parked and went in.

Oh, my God! I was so scared, but I walked into the reception area.

A lady came up to the counter and asked, "How can I help you?"

"I would like to complete an application," I replied.

"Are you here in answer to our ad?"

"I didn't know that you were running an ad."

"Well, do you have a resumé?"

"Yes," I smiled," I do."

"Well, let me see your resumé and you can read our ad."

I felt like such a greenhorn, trying to be businesslike. Who was I kidding?

Everything listed in the ad as an experience requirement and skill was on my resumé! I completed the application and handed it to the woman. Another answer to prayer!

"Let us look at this. I will call you."

The next day, I got the call; and I had a job!

The business was a family corporation which manufactured airplane wing assemblies for all the big airplane companies. In the front office were Leona, CEO and family mother; Bobbie, who I had met on inquiry day, the eldest daughter and who acted as office manager; Lillian, called Lil, who did payroll; Ted, the eldest son, who held the title of president; Don, middle son and vice president; Tom, the younger son whose job title I never did learn; Betty, the phone answerer; and later, Marilyn, receptionist/typist; and Diane, youngest, who came in once in a while. I think that she was a stay-at-home mom at the time. Her husband, also on payroll, did run-about jobs.

Leona, Lee as we called her, was ruler over all that was going on. My desk was about six feet from hers; and I could not help but overhear her telling people on the phone, "I'm just here to cause hate and discontent." She thought that that was a great joke. I came to learn that she was a pretty angry, bitter, 75-year-old lady.

Lil did detailed accounting compared to what I had done in the past. After I worked for the company for a while, I did payroll when Lil was not at work.

My job, "Job Cost Accounting," was to keep account of every expense that went into each individual wing assembly. This included the hours of every worker who spent any time on any individual part of each wing assembly. This kind of bookkeeping was new to me. I found it to be interesting, and I really liked doing it. Making that bottom-line balance each time intrigued me greatly! I also reconciled the company checkbook monthly. This company's running balance was one million dollars, way different from the balances that I had worked with at Verda Cattle Company!

No such thing as an ESP (error some place) journal entry existed here to make it balance. In the past, that was my option if my business' balance was a few cents off.

Ted's wife, Betty, came in afternoons to be at the front desk and answer the phones. Later another lady was hired to work that job fulltime along with typing any necessary documents. Marilyn became a good friend to me.

During that time, mornings, while getting ready for work, I always listened to Christian radio. I especially found two programs to inspire and be a good way to begin my day. Somehow, in conversation, I learned that Bobbie listened to the same programs. Sometimes we talked about what we had heard. I guess by our conversation the rest of the office knew that I was a Christian. I had never done any so-called "witnessing." Hopefully, I was wearing an attitude and lifestyle that gave them that idea. I truly think that God "armed me" just as I had asked Him to do.

The office was one large room with our desks placed along the outer wall, all facing inward in a big circle. Therefore, our conversations were in no way ever private, but rather easy conversation across the room as we worked. The business was dysfunctional, but the conversation much more so!

It was during my first week there that Don, the middle son, came over to Lee's (his mom's) desk and said something to her quietly. I wasn't paying much attention until he was walking past my desk saying to her, "Go look in the parking lot."

The next day Lee told Bobbie that she and Ted were going to look at new cars. I was a bit slow, but I finally put it together. Don was telling his mom to look at my car, a Mercedes. To this day, I fail to see of what interest or consequence that was to them. It was not a new car, probably six years old; however, it was pretty, with fancy spoke wheels.

One day while working I noticed that Lil and Lee were watching me like hawks. I had given them no indication that I was incompetent or untrustworthy, so I could not imagine any reason for their behavior. Their actions spoke loud and clear, and that day as well as many others I went home crying and wondering how to handle it.

I always got up extra early to have time to read my Bible and have my prayer time. One morning, my reading was expressing that I should be confident, putting on the full armor of God. I don't recall the exact reference; there are a few such. This was an eye opener for me. I prayed that and each morning thereafter, asking God to arm me with confidence and not let their comments and looks break through. I began to walk into that office and not allow their comments to get to me! Also, my attending a 10-week class, "From Doormat to Dynamic," was helping me to gain self-worth.

I had also noticed that when a colorful joke was passed from desk to desk it failed to reach mine. I wondered about that, but let it go. In my devotion time one morning, the word "sanctified" stood out to me from my Bible reading. It was like God was saying to me, "You are one of those that has been sanctified."

I instantly opened the dictionary waiting next to me, as always when I read, and looked up the word. I found it meant that I had been set apart. I realized that while I must live in this world, I would not need to be a part of some of the activities that go on in it. Wow! This really spoke to me. Just because there was bad language or off-color things going on, maybe okay for others, I need not be a part of it. With that in mind, I realized that others not sharing their jokes with me was somehow a compliment to my character. This thought made me feel better. I was different, I knew it, and I would not look back. I mention this because of what happened several years later.

Something that I was necessarily a part of was when Ric and Karen's relationship showed its true colors.

It was a Thursday in 1986, and the pay phone at the AA center in California where I had just opened and prepared coffee for the meeting rang. I picked up. It was Ric, in Arizona; and he was crying.

"What's the matter, Honey?" I asked.

"It's Karen. She's gone."

"Where has she gone?"

"I don't know, Mom. Karen's gone, with the baby; the kids are crying, and asking for her. I don't know what to do."

"Can I call you when I get home?" I asked.

"Yeah. I have to work tonight. What do I do? I can't leave the kids alone while they're sleeping, can I?"

"Don't you know of anyone who can help tonight?"

"The only person I can think of is Jimmy." Jimmy was a single neighbor of Ric and Karen's, who was in the same business as we were.

I assured him that we would figure something out, and we hung up.

Only after hanging up could I even conceive of the reality of it. I knew that our small family system, which had revealed cracks, was now truly broken; but I did not yet know to what extent. Ric worked nights and should have been able to sleep for his job, but he was now home without his wife wondering what next. Karen's leaving had come as a complete surprise to me, and maybe to Ric also. Ric had initially found Karen as a runaway. And now, she had run again.

Initially, Jimmy did watch the kids for a few nights. Then, at my suggestion, we brought the kids to California for a trip to visit Grandma Verda. They were fine with that. Vicki and I developed a tag-team approach, me dropping them off at Vicki's when I went to work; her watching them through the day (along with her own three); and me picking them up there in the evening for dinner and baths. This worked reasonably well. Several months later, approaching time for school to resume—which would be his older daughter's beginning to kindergarten, and their father now exhibiting high mania and suspicious paranoia—Ric asked us to send them back. We did, but hesitantly. How could he handle all that was now solely his responsibility?

Being without baby sister and Mommy was a great loss. We each offered our best, but how could that fill in for Mommy being gone? The children coped and reacted as best they could, which also involved varying degrees of blaming their father. When he was clear-headed enough to do so, he told them that he loved them and that Mommy would be back when she felt better.

As it turns out, Karen never "felt better" about her and Ric's marriage. Her leaving Ric was forever; and, for two of their three children, the time apart from her was traumatic. Maybe others would say that he or I should have seen it coming. I cannot say if he did or not, but I do not think so. He probably should have because it turns out that domestic violence caused the rift. But his thinking was also thwarted by great work and domestic pressure and alcohol troubles of his own.

I loved Ric, Karen, and their family; and I wanted to help. All that I could do was mention that something existed that was like a shelter for women. This was a relatively new concept back then. Thankfully, Karen qualified and went there, but just for a few days, checking herself out. Unfortunately, she was not there long enough to recognize her part in the domestic violence cycle.

Also, there was another important aspect of Karen having run away; it was what she had run to. Actually, not what, but who. Karen had a sister. And Karen's sister had a husband. The two families had been friends, raising their children as cousins who knew and loved each other, of course. But the love lines got tangled up at some point, because Karen was running from Ric to her sister's husband, Ricky.

* * *

Though Karen left Ric, it was their oldest daughter who suffered most from her parents' fighting before their separation. Understandably, her view of her dad was forever damaged. Knowing this fed Ric's depression. He was otherwise such a caring man.

To this day, as a young woman, his eldest daughter wants no dredging of memories, especially positive ones of her father. Ric and Karen's son, however, is interested in talking about his dad and wishes he had known him more.

I have told him, "I am an open book. Ask me, I will tell you."

He does ask questions, especially since he married his new wife.

I try to fill in the gaps where possible.

* * *

Four years had passed with me working at Ralee. And as that time passed, I realized that I was no longer comfortable working there. Bobbie had learned that she had breast cancer and continued working with a chemo pack attached to her body. She passed away not long after that. I had loved her much, and I missed her.

After Bobbie's funeral service, it was back to work as usual. Lee expressed no emotion but soon brought the younger daughter, Diane, to take over Bobbie's desk and job. The girl's heart was at home with her two little boys; she appeared confused about her job and was very angry. Additionally, she was not Bobbie and, in fact, was rather caustic. I decided to list my home to sell. When it did sell and escrow was opened, I made the decision to give notice and quit.

In the process, I had gone house shopping in the small town of Nuevo, near my high school friend, Sherry. I opened escrow on a new home on a quarter acre in Riverside County. I was so excited about moving into that beautiful, new, ranch-style house! Between taking Sherry, my former sister-in-law, and other friends to see the place as often as I felt that I could intrude upon the realtor, I was determining built-ins for the garage and furniture placement and purchase. Additional to that, I had also qualified to open, contingent upon the sale of my home, a Hallmark gift shop in a new shopping center being built near Nuevo. Plus, the church that I had been attending had planned a mission trip out of the country to South America, and both my realtor handling the sale of my Hacienda house and I were signed up to go! I could not have been praising God more or believing more that He was in charge of all of this! I was thrilled to be almost to the final departure from a job that brought too much pressure and negativity with it, and I was so excited to think that I could be back in business for myself!

I had trained a new gal to take my job, so I was doing some odd jobs around the office until my last day. About four days before what was to be my last day in the office, I received a call from my realtor. The message stunned me. I asked that she repeat her words. Unbelievably, the house had fallen out of escrow. Why? The buyer had experienced a death in the family in another country. Yes, the buyers were gone.

I don't think that I thanked her or said goodbye, just hung up the phone and stood unmoving. I was in shock. My heart was breaking. I had no idea what I was going to do. Everything in my house was packed in boxes stacked in the dining room and beyond, and the movers were scheduled to arrive at my door on the closing date. The rest of the day was a slow, mechanical blur.

Finishing the workday as fast as possible, I hurried away from the office feeling the unfairness of life, my disappointment co-mingling with anger. Once home, I stripped off my nice work clothes, threw myself on the bed, and cried. I yelled, sobbed, and let stream long and great boohoos. I could not muster tears enough to express my anguish.

"God, why? What am I going to do? I have no job, and I still have a mortgage! What is happening? Where do I go from here?"

Pausing, I tossed on my old sweats, reviling their look on my tired bones, thinking that I would proceed to feeling even sorrier for myself. However, the thoughts came to me that an AA meeting was going to start soon and that I needed to get there! And I did.

That is how God works in my life, if I will get out of myself and go see and be with other people.

At the meeting, I shared, almost without thinking, "I don't know what I am going to do; I guess that I'll have to rent rooms in my house." And I went home and cried some more.

I returned to that meeting the next week primarily because of, as God would have it, the previous week's "new" man, who I had never seen before. This new man, Don, got my attention, something which I had not experienced for six years! During that meeting, I mentioned to the group that I was grieving the loss of my little old, blind dog, Dulce. I shared that my granddaughter had been visiting on a day that I happened to be under the hood of my car, replacing the AC freon, again solving more life problems. Unbeknownst to me, she had let Dulce out; and Dulce had wandered down the steps of the stairway on the patio. Those stairs led to the pool area, where we found Dulce floating lifeless in the jacuzzi.

Several people at the meeting expressed sympathy, as did Don, who said that he was a dog lover. I tried to hold back my tears.

After that meeting, Don walked up to me and asked if he could talk to me. Of course! Little did I know that we were to have an audience for our conversation! That audience, watching from the 13-passenger company van that Don drove to meetings weekly, was comprised of some of his clients, required to attend meetings to stay in the recovery program. Don again mentioned sorrow for my loss, and I thanked him. Then he asked if I still planned to rent rooms in my house.

As I had forgotten that I had said that, I replied, "Gosh, I'm still not sure what I am going to do; but, you are welcome to come look and see if it would work for you." He said that he would keep thinking about the possibility.

Shortly thereafter, for July 4 weekend, I—along with Vicki and her daughter, plus several of our friends and their kids—attended our annual church camp. We loaded up our food and gear as well as Megan, my granddaughter, along with her bike and fishing pole, and drove to the large campground.

Megan's delight camping was to ride her bike back and forth between the small stream and the pool. Sitting at the stream with her tackle box and pole, every fish she caught she gently removed from the hook with her pliers and tossed back into the water. When the sun got the best of her, she straddled her bike, rode back to the pool, jumped in and refreshed, and then was off to the stream again! We each delighted in camping in our own way.

It was there, around the campfire, that I found myself admitting, "Girls, I think that I have found someone who I can love."

Their gleeful response, in unison was, "Oh, Mom!"

Back home and back at my AA meeting, I repeatedly announced sign-up for a Catalina weekend AA event and trip. I found myself really hoping that Don would register to go. No such thing happened.

Don had just begun a new job in the area and needed a place to stay three nights a week. Otherwise, he lived in Hemet, about 70 miles east, near where I had planned to move.

The next week, Don asked if he could see my place. I said, "Sure, just follow me home."

I showed him the room upstairs.

"What do you want for it, and may I begin renting it next week?"

Having lived alone quite comfortably for six years, I suddenly found this man who might live with me quite interesting. I wanted to get to know him better.

I found myself saying, "I don't see why not." And suddenly, I had a roommate!

I'm a realtor!

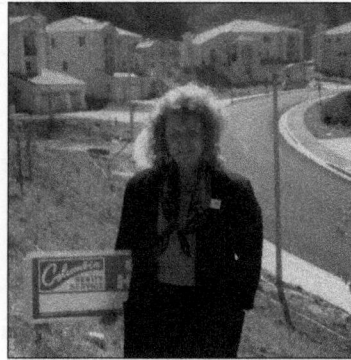

New listing.

Shortly after that, on my last day at work I was in the little kitchenette gathering my personal belongings when Lil entered. She told me that she really cared for me and was going to miss me. This and her big hug caught me by surprise. I told her that I would miss her too.

* * *

About three years later, on a Sunday morning, my phone rang. To my surprise, it was Lil, who I had not seen or talked to since that last day at work. Sounding a bit tearful and very excited, she said, "I just had to call you to tell you that I am being baptized this morning at my daughter's church!"

Surprised to hear her British accent and happy about her news, it took me a while to figure out why she wanted me to know. I now believe that it was because of all the prayer and "armor-bearing" I experienced during that time. How strange yet beautiful that conversation was, another message from God to inspire me even more. We have not spoken since.

CHAPTER EIGHTEEN

Don

After Don asked me about renting a room in my house, our friendship began. Quickly, he became a good friend; and I found myself really caring about him. Though he lived at my place, I could still have my privacy as my house was tri-level, with my bedroom downstairs and the other three upstairs.

Don's new job ran four 10-hour days, from 1:00 p.m. to 10:00 p.m.

I had always been an early-to-bed, early-to-rise kind of person. Now, I was finding myself waiting up for him so that we could talk. He was a conversational and kind guy. He knew how to keep the chat going, and it was nice to have someone to talk to. He also gave me little compliments along the way on things about me that he found interesting. Boy. That was a new concept for me.

As our friendship grew, he would say, "You are a generous lady and a woman of integrity." Or, "I like your tenaciousness." Due to his wide vocabulary, I sometimes consulted my dictionary to gain a true understanding of what he was saying. While I felt that the words were complimentary, I wanted to make sure!

Quickly, I found myself falling in love, which I had vowed to never do again! I had felt content with my single life and had long thought, "Done my time; don't need to do that again."

Because of my history, this love fall felt a bit like a roller coaster, full of fun and excitement yet sometimes overwhelming. One day I was totally "in" love; the next I was "out" in uncertainty and doubt. I now understand that while I felt that I had it together by this point and knew myself, some of my responses happened because my primary drive was lust and therefore mostly sexual. This emotional ride continued for the first year and a half after Don and I met, and the strong attraction drove me to points of confusion.

To distract myself, I started meeting men from an online service for lunch or dinner:

A retired pilot and I met at a local coffee shop, engaged in an interesting conversation for several hours, then never spoke again.

Another man was from Denmark. For several weeks he called me, and we enjoyed chatting. I never met him.

Another man, living in Thousand Oaks, took me out to The Velvet Turtle, a restaurant near my home. After a nice dinner he asked if he could see me again. Yes. Next time we met, he rode his Gold Wing motorcycle and took me to church on it before we headed to Banning for a day of apple picking at an orchard there. That was a fun day!

Don was only at my place the three nights during the week. Each Thursday evening, he went back to Hemet for the weekend. Each Monday evening, when he returned, he asked, "How was your weekend?" and I would tell him about it!

This was difficult for me as I knew that I was growing to love him. I had a little war going on within. I kept reminding myself that I had done my time. Still, I could see that he had a concern of some sort about my weekend behavior.

Don soon asked if he could rent the room full time. He said that he was growing weary of going to Hemet each weekend. I agreed to the fulltime rent.

Soon thereafter, Don stated, "I find you to be very interesting. I would like to date you."

My heart almost stopped! It was screaming "Yes!" Still, I found my mouth saying, "I'd like to date you too, but I don't know how to date someone who lives in my house."

His reply? "Well, of course, I'll have to find somewhere else to live."

Our first date.

Crazily (but I believe it was God working in my life) after Don asked me to date him, I never received another call from any other man with whom I had been conversing.

Much later, when I heard Don tell the story, he said, "Here I was, thinking that I would move from upstairs to down, and she says that I would have to move out!"

Vicki had a small travel trailer that she was not using, so she offered it as Don's possible next home. Having graciously considered that option, Don accepted for the time being.

A few months later, he asked me, "What do you think about getting married?"

Again, my heart stopped. "I can't do that."

"Talk to me," he prodded. "What can't you do? What do you think marriage requires?"

I told him that I had done my time in that department and that I could not do it again. "I don't want to do all the laundry, meal planning, and all that it takes to be a good wife. I am quite comfortable just taking care of myself."

"Why do you think that that is part of the requirements?"

"It all goes along with being a responsible wife."

Then he said, "Would you go to counseling with me?"

"Yes. I can do that."

We ended up seeing a therapist for about six months. His therapist. At the first session I sat on the low, comfy-looking sofa, thereby placing myself in a position of looking up at both the therapist and Don. I suddenly became passive and childlike, seeming to request sympathy that I did not want or need. I did not know what happened. I did not understand it.

Afterward, back in the car, and not yet having started it to leave, Don asked, "What just happened in there?"

"I have no idea," I replied. "That's not me, not anymore."

"Yeah, that was not the Verda that I know," he said. And off we went.

But I continued processing it on my own. The next session, pre-determined by myself in conversation with no one, I sat in one of the club chairs, at eye level. That made all the difference; I was back to my new, strong self—the me that I had been doing all the work to become.

At some point, while going through counseling Don had commented, "Sounds like I'm a lot like Cliff."

When I told her, my girlfriend Jackie had cautioned, "Verda, he's trying to warn you that he may not be who you think he is." I realized then that I needed strong discernment, which I thought I had by then. I had written in my pink journal, "I feel like I have it together now."

Whether I did or not, through the course of our counseling meetings I became more confident that I could indeed be a wife again.

One day standing at the kitchen sink, in his characteristically unromantic way, Don asked again, "Would you consider marrying me now?" Yes, I would.

We bought the ring together, as in "Go pick out a ring, and I'll reimburse you." So, I did; and we set a date: August 9, 1992. Next, we bought a 27-foot travel trailer of which he tore out the interior bunk beds and the like to make comfy for us as newlyweds.

Remember the couple who had previously left the country, leaving me with the need to find new buyers for my house? They had at the time put down $5,000. I took the fact of their unannounced departure to small claims court, despite numerous attempts to serve the papers. I won! It was that money that we used to pay for our wedding!

Don and I both believed that God had brought us together for many reasons, and we wrote our vows related to those specifics. The wedding was simple and informal, with an open invitation to all our family and friends.

One of Don's high school buddies, Dane, owner of a major neon lighting company in Phoenix and who remodeled classic cars and showed them throughout the nation (many of which were highlighted in Hot Rod magazine), attended. He flew in directly from Kentucky rather than first returning to his home in Arizona, where he was a prominent yet casually-dressed businessman. I later learned that he had told Don that the variety of people in attendance, from street person to business owner, was thoroughly surprising to him. Also in attendance were my high school friend, Sherry, and her husband.

Ceremony, Vern singing.

Family.

Verda and Don with Vicki and Donnie.

The Bride and Groom by the river.

Vicki stood up with me, as Don's son did with him. Ric, who had been in prison until shortly before then, chose not to attend. Surprisingly, his ex-wife and her new man were present with her and Ric's children. Additionally, our therapist attended. And, so did my manicurist!

We were married on the campground along the side of a small river and served the guests a meal on the patio of the Camp Williams facility café, which was part mobile home park. People remember it as the hottest day of the year, but I recall it as the day that changed my life with a promise and commitment of love.

As we began our marriage, just being together was SO fun! It was like we were nonstop camping and playing house in our travel trailer. Don, having been a general contractor previously, tore out some of the inside to make more room for us; and we parked it in the same spot, on a hill overlooking the river, where he had originally located the smaller RV. He built a fence around the perimeter so that our dogs could be outside safely, planted a small lawn, and installed a hammock between a tree and a big post. We then planted flowers, including a strawberry plant border. Don was tickled mornings when I picked berries for him to eat with his cereal! We were as cozy as could be daily in our little corner of the world as I happily called it; and the rolling waters lulled us to sleep nightly.

We lived most of the first five years of our marriage in that 27-foot trailer while I rented all four bedrooms in my house to graduates from The River Community.

In addition to our home parked near the river, we bought a pickup truck and camper. Our vacations, beginning at the end of summer after school began, took us to places like Nevada; Idaho; Montana; Alberta, Canada; Washington; Oregon; Utah; and a large part of Arizona. Our favorite short trips were north to Avila Beach, California, at the port of San Luis; west of San Luis Obispo; or east, to the Colorado River out of Blythe, California. To carry us further on little byways, we purchased a small classic motorcycle. It was a 1969 Honda with a little 5-horsepower engine, powerful enough for us to keep up with traffic while riding together and light enough for Don to stow on a platform he added to the back of the camper.

Our simple process was to park the rig, pull the motorcycle off, and ride to any desired sights, eating establishments, and AA meetings. We rarely stayed in a campground. As each day drew to its close, Don watched both sides of the highway in the distance, looking for a promising green growth of trees. Once spotted, he commented, "There's water over there." We headed as straight for it as possible, often on a bumpy dirt road or logging road. Within several minutes we would come upon a stream or river, home for that evening. That was especially great as our small camper offered no shower. Carrying limited water, the stream washed away any dust of the day—quickly too, because that fresh water was cold!

One of my absolute favorite places we visited was Waterton Lake National Park in Alberta, Canada. There, animals including bighorn sheep, elk, and deer all grazed on the lawns and strolled through the acreage as if they owned it. An old hotel, Prince of Wales, built in the 1920s, sat on a hill overlooking the campground and adjoining village. The scene was beyond pretty.

Though Don was typically resistant to eating out, I convinced him that we have lunch there. We learned from our server, a college student like the other staff and soon headed back to school, that we were dining on the last weekend that the restaurant was open before winter. Later that afternoon, the rain began; and sometime during the night, during the silence, the snow fell. Neither of us regretted that meal, and the experience was etched as one of my treasured memories with Don.

Our great memories were so varied, another plus to our marriage. Of course, we traveled with our three dogs. One night, still at Lake Waterton, I opened the door as habitual of an evening, to take the dogs out for their last bathroom opportunity. We exited, walked just a few steps in the pitch black, heard heavy rustling sounds, and the dogs went crazy with barking. Of course, we got back to our shelter as fast as possible. Turns out that we had almost tripped on a herd of elk bedded down for the night!

Another morning in another place (possibly Idaho or Montana) I opened the door to let the dogs out only to find that we were surrounded by cattle curiously sniffing out the rig. Of course, the dogs again barked like mad, scattering the group in moments. We never knew who or what we might meet!

That was a very happy time for me. I have always loved travel and RVing. We had more fun in that little camper than I ever had in the ostentatious, 35-foot fifth wheel known in my first marriage. Off-road sights are the prettiest, and only small rigs can get to them. We spent our nights during that time in such beautiful places.

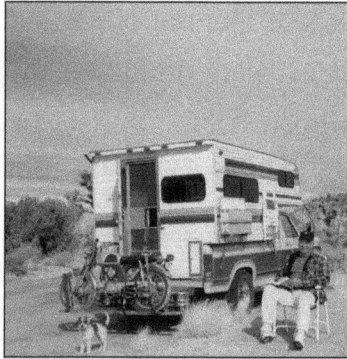

On the road again.

Don was working in the mountains and canyon above Azusa, California at The River Community Long-Term Dual-Diagnosis Recovery Facility. In a few short years, he became Director of the entire program. Related to our AA, we became active on the Hospitals and Institutions Committee. We regularly took a group of three or four sober AA people—known as a panel—(and for whom we had to get special entry clearance) into jails, prisons, and mental institutions to share personal stories with others with addiction problems. Another reason this was fitting for each and both of us was that Don worked in the field of dual-diagnosis; and my son, Ric, while incarcerated, had eventually been diagnosed with a bi-polar disorder. This form of "giving back" brought us great satisfaction and drew us together.

Later, we joined the National Alliance for the Mentally Ill (NAMI). Through that organization we enrolled in and completed training for "A Journey for Life," which prepared us to teach people how to better understand their family members living with mental illness. Don was such a good teacher, truly admired by his students.

I honestly feel that God wanted me to know that marriage could be fun and fulfilling. That was why he brought Don into my life. I learned so much from the entire experience of that marriage!

CHAPTER NINETEEN

A Deep Valley

It was August 15, 1996. Don that day, for whatever reason, had come home for lunch and just gone back to work when our house phone rang. A man asked if I had a son by the name of Donald Ric Umfleet.

Ric and me, December 1995.

"Yes, I do."

He introduced himself as Sheriff from the Tempe, Arizona, Sheriff's office.

"Are you at home alone?" he asked.

"Yes."

"Please sit down," he directed. "An accident occurred on the night of August 12. Donald was involved. He did not survive. We have been trying to reach you for a few days. We sent an officer to your home in Hacienda Heights."

I just sat there. That was my home down the mountain.

"Ma'am?"

"I don't know what to do." I did not; and that was all that I could say, over and over.

"Ma'am, is there someone you can call?"

"Yes, I can call my husband."

The Sheriff had me write his name and phone number down and said, "Have your husband call me back." And we hung up.

I quickly called for Don to come home; his business was just about a half mile down the river. I'm sure that I told his receptionist what had happened because he came right home and called the Sheriff's office.

I just sat there. I could not think. I felt utterly helpless.

The Sherriff gave Don all the accident information and outlined some next steps, including making funeral arrangements. It would take some time to bring Ric's body to California.

So unreal to me, all I could think was, "I have to see him. Then I will believe that this is real." I don't know how others who lose a loved one can experience acceptance of the death when they can't find that person's body.

The following is what had happened:

On the night of August 12, Ric, age 42, had been drinking. It was after 9:00 p.m. and he was out riding his bicycle. He had been staying at his former neighbors' Rich and Donna's house, sleeping on their sofa and appreciating their friendship.

In the opinion of the police, he was homeless. Ric did not feel that he was homeless because he had a storage unit filled with his furniture and personal belongings. The managers of the storage facility later told us that they saw him there on numerous occasions. One Sunday afternoon he was barbequing with a woman and watching a football game on TV. The storage manager commented, "Ric was such a likable guy, we just looked the other way."

According to the police report, the twenty-nine-year-old woman who hit and killed Ric (we will call her Cindy) stated that she had picked up some food at Jack in the Box after leaving the bar where she had been attending a pool tournament. As she drove, she was reaching toward the passenger floor of the car to get something out of the bag of food. She stated that her car must have gone toward the bike lane. She did not see Ric riding his bicycle, and she hit him; he was crossing the street on a dark road.

Cindy agreed to take the breath test at the scene; it read her to be over the legal alcohol limit. She was arrested and charged with negligent manslaughter. Over two hours later, when her blood was drawn, it was below the limit. She was released.

Cindy had been driving her mother's new BMW. The insurance company considered the vehicle a total loss. She hit Ric while speeding. The report stated that his tissues were found on the inside rear window of that car. Ric's death was her second event coming from the same bar. As the first was past the statute of limitation, it could not be considered in this collision with Ric.

When the Sheriff called to tell me her charges, I questioned, "And she can go to a four-hour drivers' class, and it will not appear on her record?"

"Unfortunately," he replied, "that is the case."

"And my son went to prison and lost three years of his children's lives because of his drinking and driving. Yet, he never hurt or killed anyone!"

Previously, at some point in our conversation related to our pending case with Cindy, the Prosecutor had asked me why Ric went to prison. I told her that it was because he had too many drinking and driving citations. She informed me, "People don't go to prison for drinking and driving."

"Then I want to know why he was in prison."

"Are you sure you really want to know, because I can find out for you."

"Yes, I really want to know."

Later, she called me about the answer. I was correct. Ric served three years because of his drinking and driving. I knew my son was not a hardened criminal. But knowing that could not bring him back!

Now I had a choice: I could get bitter and hateful toward the unfairness of the judicial system and this woman for the rest of my life, OR I could pray for her and hope she finds Alcoholics Anonymous.

The Sheriff gave Don and me her address. We chose to write a note to let her know that we were praying for her. Don wrote it; I mailed it.

She never replied.

I don't know if she ever got help.

I still pray for her.

* * *

When Don called his mom, Mary (I called her Mom Mary) to tell her what had happened, she said, "Don, you need to call Tom." Tom was formerly a kid from a family who had been prominent members of Don's dad's church, and Tom's dad now lived down the hall from Mom Mary at the Beatitudes in Phoenix.

Don said, "Mom, I haven't seen Tom since we were kids."

Unfortunately, Tom was not available. He had already been retained by the drunk girl's family. We hired a different attorney to represent us.

One day, still handling Ric's affairs, he called me about the future of Ric's children. As they were still minors, he explained, he could not act immediately on their behalf as I had requested. He could pay our expenses, he told me.

"However," he encouraged, "when Ric's ex-wife, their mother, calls us we can easily set up a trust fund for his children."

That was something great to hear in this darkness. I let Karen know that all she had to do was call the attorney to get the kids' future security set up.

"Not happening," she replied.

I could not believe my ears. "What do you mean, no?"

"Ricky says no; if not all of the kids can get something, then none can."

As not all of Karen's children were from her and Ric's union, those children obviously could not be included. While I agreed that that was unfortunate, my thinking was that helping some of them would help them all.

My thinking was not invited.

There was simply nothing further that I could do about that circumstance.

This bothered me then as it does now, though I try to leave it lie in my head. Years later I see my grandchildren struggling to get their starts in life. I still wonder what else I could have done to persuade her, but she was under the influence of control.

Later, the Prosecutor told me that Tom was at that time the most powerful defense attorney in the state of Arizona. I feel that the Prosecutor did not want to go up against him in court. She also told me that Cindy's dad had a lot of money, lived in Orange County, and had hired Tom. Since my son was considered "homeless and indigent" there was not much chance that she could win the case.

It was never mentioned that Ric had been a Corpsman in the U.S. Navy, with honorable discharge. Nor did it surface that he became a certified phlebotomist. He was a man who happened to have the problem and disease of alcoholism as well as diagnosed bipolar disorder. Such became the case for many Vietnam veterans, who were discounted—in my opinion, given no credit or help for anything because they didn't win a war. I only wish that I had had the presence of mind to bring up those facts.

Shortly after Ric's death, before his body had even been released from Arizona and sent to California, Don was required to attend an educational conference in San Diego at the Hotel Coronado. Though I felt somewhat out of touch, I did not want to be left alone in our little trailer; so, I requested to join him. He agreed that I should go.

Once at our destination, I realized that I had left all our clothes for the weekend at home in our garment bag. Because he had to get to his classes, I drove alone to a large discount store similar to what we today call a Walmart. Inside, I found that I could not focus. I needed to talk, so I spoke to a customer standing looking in the same area where I was.

"I just can't think; I lost my son this week."

A puzzled look on her face, she replied, "What are you doing here?"

"Well, my husband is attending a work conference here and I went off without any of our clothes. They're hanging near our front door in the garment bag, right where I left them."

She wished me the best, I somehow got what we needed, and I returned to the hotel.

I made it through the weekend, but I recall little more about it than that event.

Grieving Ric took a while.

That season was interrupted again by another event. This time, just weeks after Ric's funeral, we were asked to be keynote speakers at an Al-Anon/AA weekend retreat in the mountains, all accommodations and meals provided. I talked about Al-Anon and how it worked for me, and Don shared about

AA and his experiences. Speaking to others about each of our personal stories with alcohol and addiction was a privilege.

We had received many such invitations, but this one was particularly poignant. A sober husband and wife, a son lost due to someone else's drunk driving, and the chosen hope of tomorrow.

Though it took a while, I have chosen to live with a free spirit of forgiveness without bitterness. I wish that these hard circumstances and events had never happened. However, I love the freedom that I live with because of the forgiveness that God has given me. Thank you, God!

If you have experienced such a life event, which I hope that you never do, I would like to remind you that holding on to that departed person only keeps you stuck and hurts you and eventually wounds those around you. Won't you consider surrendering that hurt and trusting your life to God today? And when you do, you will let that person rest in peace, because that person would not want to see you living in such desperate sadness.

CHAPTER TWENTY

Expectations

I have learned that when I am not feeling comfortable with myself in a conversation, especially when I am in it with some family members, it always seems to come down to the fact that either I am expecting something of a situation or person OR I am feeling that something is being expected of me, which either I cannot or feel unwilling to fulfill. And the conflict—now being taught to the young to be recognized as an "uh-oh," unsettled feeling within and later perhaps as a subconscious feeling or something conscience-related—may in my life now be my sensing that the Holy Spirit is nudging me. If you have experienced this in whole or part, you may agree. Let me explain a bit further.

Both before and after my son's divorce a few times I saw a sad look on my daughter-in-law's face and tears in her eyes, either during a greeting or goodbye. When that happened, I felt like I was not meeting an expectation that she had. I felt so uncomfortable because I imagined that she expected of me something unspoken. I could never find out if that was true because the looks or tears always happened at a time that it seemed impossible to ask her what she needed.

Another such instance took place after Don and my wedding ceremony. As I mentioned, unexpectedly my former daughter-in-law and her new husband had traveled all the way from Arizona with my three grandkids. At the end of the ceremony, as some moved toward the reception after congratulating us (and while many others still crowded around) I hugged Karen and thanked her for bringing the children. The response that she gave, in facial expression and with tearing eyes, resulted in me feeling awkward. Unfortunately, with all those people right there, we had no privacy; and I could not take time out to speak with her alone. I always wondered what she wanted from me in that moment that I could neither discern nor give.

Another expectation situation that I recall took place during my marriage to Don. I was planning to attend a weekend women's retreat. I had asked Don if he would drop me off at the home of the lady who was going to drive us so that I would not need to leave my car on her street. He easily agreed. On the Friday departure morning, me still in bed, Don informed that he was not going to be able to drop me off as planned. This was not the first time that this had occurred; he had a habit of telling me that he would do something, then not following through. Most of the time I could understand and make another plan.

This day I instead laid there in bed, stewing. Not yet fully awake, I guess that information caught me off guard. I let him know, through body language and severe tone of voice that I noted how he often did this, leading me on in expectation.

No comment from my husband.

Shortly thereafter, I was in the bedroom sitting on the bed still waiting for my turn in the bathroom where he was still shaving while my mouth ran on.

On a wall across the hall between the two rooms hung a large picture in a glass frame. I happened to be looking at it when I saw Don give me the finger!

"I saw that!" I said, with emphasis.

Don jumped and hastily looked around in complete shock.

In a state of "self-rightness" I completed my readying, then went to the kitchen. There, I had some time alone to think about the episode, and I knew that I owed amends. Then, it struck me as intensely funny that he had turned around as he did. I went to him before we had our morning prayer.

"Don, I am sorry for my outburst. I understand how busy you are at this time."

Don had recently taken more on with this new position of Director where he worked and was really on overload. He had continued with all previous responsibilities and added additional, including all the involved time for additional paperwork.

"I had been holding an expectation of you unfairly. I understand that it simply does not work for you to drop me off."

"Oh, Sweetheart. Thank you. And I am sorry for my childish response."

We had a chuckle, prayed together, he left for work; and then I prepared for my retreat. As it turned out, my friend had me park my car in her driveway. All was well.

The next day, Saturday, Don was to pick up cakes that I had ordered for his buddy's sobriety anniversary party, though I could not be there myself. I did not think another thing about that or our disagreement because we had prayed; Don however, did.

While at the retreat, Saturday evening I went against the rules and called Don.

He said, "I've got a surprise for you." Then I heard him say, "Wait! Where did he go? Oh, there he is. "

I asked, "Who's he?"

Having given away the surprise, Don had to explain. When the party was over, Don had gone to our sober house, where my kitty, Boogie was, to check in on him. While there, he managed to capture him in a large trash can; then transported him to our condo, where I had wanted him to be all along. Boogie, a curious, tuxedo-marked cat with a prominent black spot on his nostril (thereby the name), had the "BeJeebers" scared out of him by the wild move. I loved Don all the more for this wonderful surprise—and all thanks, technically, to him giving me the finger!

But not all marital conflict had fared so well. As I reflect on my life, I see that my entire 30-plus years' marriage to Cliff had been full of expectations, trying to change who he was. I had really wanted him to read my mind. Now, I can see that he was what he was; I ought to have just walked away or adjusted to the fact. I neither saw that nor knew how to do it.

I thought then that I truly loved that man. I know now that I was in love with my dream of who I wanted him to be.

This was just another (BIG) example of, "We don't do better 'til we know better."

I am so grateful that I have become teachable. Being teachable has changed my life. However, this area remains a work in progress for me with my daughter, Vicki. I cannot determine if I have an expectation of her or if, perhaps, she has an expectation of me. Maybe the truth is that expectations exist on both sides of the relationship.

Certainly, a sense of friction exists that we cannot seem to connect through. I think that we are both aware of this friction; we just cannot yet identify its cause or know how to make a way through it. Just as when two magnets repel each other rather than come together, this energy barrier keeps us apart. This occupies my mind more than I think that it ought to; and it takes more energy doing that than I really have, or so it feels. My desire is that we could feel free with one another, without being on guard about saying something that will offend one of us or hurt either of our feelings.

This friction started after my daughter began seeing a therapist around late 1984. The therapist called a meeting that Cliff and I as well as Vicki and her husband attended. It soon became apparent to Cliff that the meeting's purpose was for Vicki to address her father about that molestation that had happened to her, by him, when she was a kid. Vicki's therapist had told her that this confronting was necessary to her life progress.

As she spoke, Cliff got defensive and blurted, "If you call that molestation, I'm doing that with —— right now!" (This child shall not be named here out of respect for privacy.)

Unbeknownst to Cliff, the therapist—by law—had to report the confession. Soon thereafter, Cliff was arrested; later, he was placed on the sexual offender list. Understandably, though we had had no part in the planning, Cliff thought that the rest of us had set him up for what happened at that meeting. Of course, we had had no idea that a second molestation was to be confessed before us all that day.

Cliff was picked up from our home the next day, arrested without my knowledge. I learned about it through his call telling me to go get him out of there. I did not even have time to process my own feelings or plan a response before he was running life again.

Naturally, habitually doing what I was told, I went to pick Cliff up. I simply saw no other option at the time. As we drove away from the jail, I asked Cliff, "What were you thinking?"

"What do you mean?" Cliff asked. Then he dared to tell me that it was his own grandchild asking questions that got things going.

"What?! If she had questions about sexual things, why didn't you tell her to ask her own mother?"

"I just didn't want her to have to learn the way I did, behind some garage, out in the open, not knowing what was happening to her."

"You really believe that, don't you, Cliff? You couldn't be more wrong. You were the adult in the situation, and not a teacher assigned to educate her about her sexuality."

Cliff insisted that it was our granddaughter's questions and his simple "helping" show- and-tell that had landed him incarcerated.

We rode on in silence the rest of the way. This was rare. I was simply dumbfounded. This disgusting talk and action was coming from my own husband.

And then, there was the huge assumption about my daughter, that through our love we would always be close. Not long after the counselor meeting and Cliff's arrest, Vicki told me that her therapist had told her that she needed to not see me for a year.

I replied, "Honey, whatever it takes for us to get healthy!"

At the same time, my heart was breaking.

I am so grateful that Vicki did not stop my granddaughters from seeing me. Maybe it was because of that that she did not stay away for an entire year. And throughout the "not seeing you" time we all continued doing family activities together. These included Christmas, church, camping, and other fun group activities. My thinking was, "I will simply continue to enjoy what we do have." Still, that year was the invisible beginning of the two large magnets pushing against one another.

Then, in 1986, on Mother's Day, Vicki informed me, "Mother's Day is my day now." She told me that she and I would no longer spend that time together either. I do not think that she was in any way trying to hurt me; she was simply informing me that that was her day now.

So, there I stood. No set plans had turned into no plans at all. Her family drove away, the friction growing, the love a question mark. I felt sad that day. For years after, I made other plans, usually spending the day with my friend, Fran.

Vicki did take part in my wedding to Don. He found it strange that I never received a card from Vicki for my birthday; and he asked about it every year.

As of this writing, Vicki calls me about every six weeks. "How are you feeling?" she asks.

I try to answer without being a whiny mother. I think that neither of us feels comfortable or vulnerable enough to share many feelings.

After our hellos, I always ask how the kids are. At first, when I did not do that, the conversation fell silent. With that question, she seems free to speak a bit. Otherwise, I am not sure that we would be able to make conversation together. I know that God has a plan for us; I just need to not hold expectations.

CHAPTER TWENTY-ONE

Another Deep Valley

Don was providing all instruction about repairs, additions to, and renovation of the old, barracks-type buildings on the River Community property. This gave the facility residents work experience that they would need to re-enter daily living. Such a good teacher, Don trained these men—who suffered mental health issues in addition to their addictions—with skills for life. One example of success was David, who mentored under Don to the point of later becoming a general contractor himself. Another young man, Senor Munoz, with extreme schizophrenia, built a successful landscape business while caring for his new wife's young child.

Don held meetings weekly at three transitional, independent-living houses for which he had initiated the idea (and I had helped to locate) and had then personally negotiated for with the owners. He remained on top of delegating other aspects of the houses, taught "Journey for Life," and drove 100 miles each way several evenings a week to attend classes in San Bernardino. The college attendance was about Don obtaining additional credits to complete his degree related to changing laws and requirements. He was on total overload.

For that reason, in June 1998 we sold the trailer and closed on a little condo down the hill in Azusa, to save him from going so far for those classes.

Then, in October 1998 Don's workplace Board, of Social Model Recovery Systems, Inc., promoted him to Director, which he had initially resisted. We were also busy planning our second "Journey for Life" group for January 1999. I had all arrangements and enrollments in place. Don's college graduation was slated for June 1999. One year seemed to be closing with promise of the next; and we were ready! And, though still somewhat overloaded, we were happy about all of it!

It was Friday, December 18, 1998. We began that day with morning prayer as each morning before starting our day.

"God, thank you for helping Verda recover from her loss of Ric, and continue to help her," was part of Don's prayer for me that morning. So good.

Don left for work, and I went to my Al-Anon group where I was the speaker. My next task for the day was grocery shopping for our Sunday dinner. This was to be Christmas dinner for our family in California because we were going to leave the following morning for Arizona in the already packed and prepped camper. The plan was that in Phoenix we would have Christmas with Don's 89-year-old mom who still lived at Beatitudes Assisted Living. From there we would spend a couple of days at our favorite place on the Colorado River.

My day was full. And everything was in order according to our and my plans.

By 9:00 p.m., however, I was perturbed. Don had not come home for dinner, and it was getting late. Then, the phone rang. It was a call for him from one of our associates from NAMI. Naturally, I told him that I would have Don return his call.

I called Don's office and the person who answered informed me, "He's up in his office; I'll have him call you." Don's office was up the hill in a different building, so someone would have to deliver the message. I continued trying to watch TV in our bed, but Don did not call; and I found myself getting really disturbed. An hour passed.

Then, at 10:00 p.m., I heard a knock on the door. Startled, I called out, "Who is it?"

"Azusa Sheriff's Department."

What?

Then Don's boss, Jim, spoke. "Verda, it's Jim."

I went to the door and let the men in, forgetting that I was just wearing one of Don's big, baggy tee shirts. Somehow, I was able to comprehend, Don was gone.

Ric had passed two years before. Yet, once again an officer is telling me that I have lost someone I dearly love. Don's belongings placed on a desk outside the restroom in his office, Don had obviously been preparing to leave to come home when he fell backward. His employee, Guy, unable to get him to answer the locked door of his office building, looked in the window and saw him lying on the floor. A former student of psychology and trained in CPR by Don himself, Guy bashed in the window and attempted to save him; he was too late.

Once again, I hear myself saying, "I don't know what to do." To me, it felt like I had just played this awful scene the week before. One officer sat at my dining room table taking notes as he asked me questions. I sat on the sofa answering about how Don was feeling when he left for work and the like. I recounted how I had asked Don to stay home because he was having a severe headache, unusual for him. As Don had no health issues that I knew of, an autopsy would be done.

And then I was alone again. Just me, in Don's baggy tee shirt, in our bed, without Don.

Everything from the couple of days that followed was a blur, and I felt that I simply could not think. I notified his son, Donnie, from Orange County. He came out to help. Together we managed to accomplish arranging Don's funeral services; I made all the necessary calls, including to Don's sister, Carol, in New York. I told Carol that I did not know how to tell his mom.

"Don't worry, Verda. I will fly there and tell her in person before we all meet for the service." Carol's husband, Roy, was also planning to attend, as was their son, who lived in Washington State at the time.

The time was short. I planned Don's service for before Christmas, recalling how hard it was when Mom had died on December 21 all those years ago and we had waited to hold the service until after the holiday. It had been like reopening a deep wound all over again, after pretending to have had a "Merry Christmas."

Don's service was standing room only. Even one of his four ex-wives attended, complimenting me, believe it or not, on the casket. "It's so fitting for Don."

A few evenings later, as I sat in bed wondering how I would possibly accomplish Christmas dinner and all the attending requirements, I saw a champagne ad in the newspaper. I thought to myself, "Tomorrow I am going to go buy a couple bottles. No one needs to know, and it will help me make it through decorating the tree and these last hurdles of 1998." With that, I went straight to sleep.

The next morning, I awoke with a laugh. I had not bothered to think about two glasses, but two BOTTLES of champagne. In the kitchen I continued my laugh and conversed with God, "Yes, God! Thank you that I never even considered a single glass of champagne. Yes, You and I both know that that would have never done the trick." As I got myself ready for a meeting, I considered that God had spared my sobriety with that thinking.

I shared my thought process in the meeting; everyone laughed, and I remained sober.

As for Don's passing, I cannot recall much of the Christmas Day that followed. I know that I revised our already-written Christmas letters and sent them out. I also managed to have the gifts and dinner at our little condo. And I got to an AA meeting right away, followed immediately by getting a new sponsor. The only feeling I experienced was numbness. Again.

I do recall the Mother's Day after Don's departure. I was keenly aware that God was with me and for me; unfortunately, my good friend Fran had lost her sobriety. From a human standpoint I was completely and obviously alone, more than ever.

A month later, having lived there exactly two years, I sold the condo. My financial advisor later explained that I had sold at the exact required time to obtain a great tax break. I had had no awareness about that. I consider that a gift from God during a deeply dark time that, due to my two huge personal losses, was otherwise unreal.

CHAPTER TWENTY-TWO

My Trip to the East Coast

Dick.

Mississippi River, New Orleans.

Biltmore Mansion, Asheville NC.

Ryman Auditorium, Nashville TN.

Birth home of MLK, Atlanta GA.

It was the latter part of 2000. The millennium and the Y2K news scare were just behind us; the world was still wondering what was going to happen in our cyber system. Literally, what on earth was going to happen?

In my part of the world, I had finally finished renovation of the Hacienda Heights house. As God would have it, I moved back there to live with Vicki and one other renter.

At AA, the man who had formerly been Don's sponsor, Dick, was planning a second trip across the country to continue investigating his family history. The previous year, his sister had joined him; she could not this year as she was in process of cancer treatments. I expressed sorrow about his sister's situation.

Later, having thought about the trip possibilities, I asked him how he would feel about me joining him. I had always wanted to see some of this beautiful country in which we live, including plantation homes in the South, of which I had read so much. "How would you feel about that?" I asked.

He thought about it, called me, and said that he saw no reason why I couldn't go along. Could I take my car, he asked, rather than his? I had no problem with that, so we began making plans.

Dick and I were to be traveling the entire month of February 2001, and I was eager!

I was also clear about one specific aspect of the trip: platonic interaction. ONLY AND EVER during the upcoming month. My intention was that I would be traveling, finally, with a male friend, with no romantic interweavings. My love with Don had fulfilled that void for me; and I had no plan to shoot holes into the fabric of my being with careless thought, sentiment, or behavior. I made that clear.

Dick and I agreed that while we were taking my car, he would pay for all fuel. At his suggestion, we agreed to share the cost of eating, with him buying one day and me the next.

"And," he proposed, "to save money, how about we share the expense of one room with two beds?"

"That all works for me!" I replied happily.

All was agreed, and off we went.

The first day we stopped in Phoenix and had lunch with my granddaughter, Amber. If I recall, I had to wrap up some business with the sale of my ranch there.

Next, in Tucson, we met with some friends of Dick's and went to an AA meeting with them.

Naturally, being scarcely acquainted, we talked a lot through the early miles of our journey. At one point he told me lightly that he did not know how this was going to go, that he had told his sponsor he might be a week into the trip and decide to return home.

"Why is that?" I asked laughing.

"Since my divorce years ago, I have never traveled with a woman except my sister."

"Oh. Okay."

Next stop was Carlsbad Caverns in New Mexico. I had my AAA information about various desired sights to see, and he had his own agenda.

Dick's plans mostly included stops in towns and cities where he had reason to believe that people related to him might have lived. He was visiting the archives at libraries in search of names connected to his. The ancestry.com site was not yet in handy existence on the Internet back then.

Another frequent stop for Dick along the way was casinos on riverboats. At the time, they could be found on most large rivers. I visited a few with him, but the smoke everywhere and loud bells ringing almost incessantly was not my thing. This was despite Dick offering me money to "play with." I had never gambled before, and to me it seemed a waste of time and money. He did not see it that way, of course.

Dick enjoyed rising before daybreak, which I do not. So, at my suggestion, he headed to the casino when one was near while I enjoyed rising a bit more leisurely. This allowed for my devotional time—reflection, prayer, and reading the Bible to consider Jesus and God in the world and how my life related. The schedule we had for mornings worked out for both of us.

Evenings along the way we attended AA meetings in the towns where we stopped for the night. A couple of nights were spent outside of Dallas in Plano. From there, Dick headed to an archive in Oklahoma while I stayed and enjoyed the pool and simple relaxation time. As my energy runs low, that was a great way to catch up on rest.

I have long savored the history of "the old South," mostly through reading related stories and books. Because of that bent, I wanted to visit related points of interest. I appreciated greatly when we did. I happened to be driving the day that we got as far as Mississippi and followed the road toward New Orleans. That stretch of road, which we were traversing in the early morning, stands out in my mind. The little townships that we passed through and places where we stopped were like going back in time.

In Vicksburg, Mississippi, we walked down a dock and met some "good ol' boys" admiring some huge catfish that they had just caught. The fish were fat and two or three feet long each!

Listening to Dick visiting with them made it feel like we were still fighting the Civil War, and that was reinforced as we saw battlefields and cannons throughout the area! Having lunched in Vicksburg, we drove through the area and on to Natchez, my mouth agape at the rich history expressed through beautiful mansions, stately library, and old courthouse. Colorful flowers abounded. Those two towns share a grandfathered law that disallows building of any kind. No supermarkets were to be found, for example. I would have so liked to enter a home in the area, and I simply did not want to leave. However, it was late in the day and all museum homes were closed. We headed down the road to find a place to stay for the night.

The next day, though it was raining, we did come upon several old structures, one an old courthouse, open to visitors. Dick joined me in visiting these and enjoyed himself. We had such a great time that we scarcely noticed how wet we were, including my dripping mess of hair, as we got back in the car and on the road again! We lunched in Biloxi on another old riverboat, then drove to New Orleans, where we stayed for a couple nights.

I thoroughly appreciated the variety of music we heard as we walked down Bourbon Street one wet and rainy evening, and Dick suggested a ride in one of the horse-drawn carriages. I declined as I was leery of anything that might suggest romance. I wanted that feeling in such a place, but it was not there for me with Dick; and I recalled my intention from prior to our trip.

The following day we walked the waterfront and had breakfast in a café along the way. We then took a streetcar out to the colonial district, thrilling me to the core again! I have long imagined returning with Vicki.

Down the road, in Atlanta, Georgia, Dick spent time at the library in city archives and I spent time viewing history by car and foot. First, I got a bit lost in a not-so-nice part of town; I just kept driving until I got to a better area. There, I learned that, among other interesting homes, Martin Luther King's family home had been restored. As we were spending a couple days in the vicinity, I invited Dick to join me in visiting that and several notable sites on the same street. We both appreciated Atlanta thoroughly.

Next stop was Savannah, where we took a bus tour. Lunch took place, upon recommendation of the tour guides, in a quaint historic restaurant.

Up the coast, in South Carolina at Myrtle Beach Dick took a picture of me sitting on a rail looking out at the ocean. Amber, my granddaughter, loved that picture so much that she framed it and has it on display in her home to this day!

All along the way, Dick continued stops to review archives and I continued touring towns and old buildings in and near the towns. On Dick's agenda for us was a boat tour in Charleston and visiting Fort Sumter.

In North Carolina, near the Great Smoky Mountains where a friend of Dick's lived, we visited a place on my wish list, the

Biltmore Estate in Asheville. I cannot describe the magnificence of that place except to mention the ongoing walking and gawking, jaw dropping. That part of the country is so pretty; and while it is another place that I have always wanted to re-visit (and preferably with my daughter), I am fairly sure that my legs would not meet the test today. Yet, the memories do not fade!

85th birthday with great granddaughter.

Next, in Nashville, Tennessee, we posed in front of the Ryman Auditorium, the premier concert and event destination of the area, and for some, of the nation! I did not think to try the door, though I was told since that the doors are always left open. I did get a picture in front, looking up at Hank Williams. We also visited the Country Music Hall of Fame and Museum. Though I know we did stop in Memphis, memory of it escapes me. Branson, Missouri, on the other hand, does stand out. That would be another intentional re-visit if possible!

One rainy day (I think it was around Springfield, Missouri), to continue Dick's family research project, we set off to drop him at the local library; however, we found it closed, possibly due to the weather. Returning to the motel, I, thinking that he might suggest a movie or such, asked, "Well, with the library not an option, what DO we want to do today?"

Dick sat there for a minute and then quietly said, "I'd like to go to bed with you."

My mind was so far from that idea that I must have gasped! I darted into the bathroom, and I prayed! Exiting a few minutes later, I responded, "I can't do that Dick; I don't love you in that way."

I knew that hurt his feelings; however, I cannot have a sexual encounter just for the sake of having sex. I had learned that when a physical encounter happens it changes the entire relationship. It brings about expectations that will eventually pull the relationship apart if not met.

The atmosphere was filled with tension, and I have no idea what we did the rest of that day.

As we continued our travel, headed toward Santa Fe, New Mexico, the mood continued a bit strained for a day or two; but as we simply went along, it got better. I think that he had called his sponsor and had a talk. That's what we do in AA to keep our balance and focus.

I wanted to stop in Taos after Santa Fe. Unfortunately, the brake light on my car lit up so we turned back to Santa Fe to get it repaired, necessarily dropping the Taos idea. Our next stop was Los Alamos as Dick wanted to visit the birthplace of the atomic bomb.

In Arizona we visited the Grand Canyon. Spending a night in Sedona, Arizona, related to that visit, we continued to Prescott. Outside of Wickenburg a "dude ranch" advertised "Lunch Being Served." Down that little road we enjoyed the final lunch of our trip.

In all, we entered 14 southern states, going to AA meetings all along the way. Part of the fun of those meetings is the format piece wherein attendees are asked, "Is anyone from out of town?"

Replying that we were from southern California almost always resulted in an offer for us to share what brought us to that meeting. The feeling of having everywhere friends who welcome and understand is something I truly cherish.

The three places in that trip that I would like to someday re-visit— this time with my daughter—are New Orleans, Branson, and Asheville.

The trip of a lifetime for me, I would also like to experience another such through the northeast part of our country. While I have never had any longing to visit other countries, I would still like to see so much more in this great USA!

EPILOGUE

How It Was, What Happened, and How It Is Now

I was much protected from the "World Outside the Church," mostly by my mother. Even as a child I had a desire to know what "that world" was made of and what it looked like. I had friends at school who did not go to church, and I liked them. I could see no difference between my friends at church and my school friends. Moving into adolescence and early adulthood, my impression was similar, except that it appeared to me that they were possibly having more fun in the world than I was.

Then, in my later 20s, driving down that dirt road on Chub's ranch, completely distraught, crying so that my eyelids had to catch up with my ability to see the road, I angrily challenged God, "God, I wish I never knew You. I can't live for Cliff and You too." That degree of me "giving up God" went hand in hand with an attitude change. It seemingly became easier for me to enjoy the "secular" and "fun things" without my typical care, guilt, or shame. For a while, I felt free. Our business was taking off, and I felt that I was flying. We were "successful," making money like I never knew we could. Somewhat wiser now, I no longer have any desire to be "worldly."

Alcohol adjusted my attitude in a way that seemed okay for a bit; but after 20 years of "all that fun" my attitude slowly turned. I experienced not liking myself at all. I was exhausted from pretending to be someone I wanted to be but was not; yet, I also felt on overload with no way to stop. Eventually, like a formerly wet cloth wrung out with no drop left, I no longer knew who I was. Life was no fun. It was downright ugly, and I did not like the way that I was living it.

How was it? Though I had had dreams of having a long-term, happy marriage, I had instead lived chaos. And become thoroughly addicted to alcohol. I later referenced this as, "Alcohol gave me wings to fly, then took away my sky."

What happened?

Realizing that I was exhausted from and unsuccessful in trying to figure out life on my own, I began to gradually humble myself. Watching TV commercials which advertised various programs to deal with addiction, I realized that I felt trapped. Writing some phone numbers on slips of paper, I pinned each to my bulletin board. I began to think that maybe there was something that I could do to change my life. What was really happening was that I was headed toward a decision to allow God to lead my life.

Previously I had thought that I was doing all I could for God with my tithe and volunteering at my church. I had continued self-intoxicating to the point that I wandered down my street nightly with my little dogs, staggering and crying. Then, that one night, I came to the epitome of it all. I don't know why that night, but I am so thankful for it. I HAD been doing all that I could for God, or close; but I had not allowed God to do for and in me. That night, I stumbled out in fear and fell into the arms of faith. I cried out to God, and He heard me and saved me.

From that time on, I attended not only church meetings and services, but I also attended "secular" and "fun things" that were previously out of the question because of my mom's views and experiences, not my personal convictions. I met people and went places, participating in events that I would have previously shunned as having the form of godliness without God—AA meetings in smoky rooms where my real God was now clearly showing me that my attitude and lifestyle could be changed for the better. A miracle took place as, one day at a time, my life was changed. I had left God, but God had never left me.

How is life now?

I took the risk of walking into the process of recovery. Through that I was able to eventually admit my faults and make necessary amends. That brought me through to true repentance (completely turning away from the alcohol and redemption). Today I am free!

One of my daily readings mentioned: "Rather than judgmentally telling folks what is right or wrong, show them the truth and let the grace of God convict their spirits." This helped me so much!

Other people's choices are not my business. This means freedom for me.

This morning my daily devotional ended with a question for the day: "What brings you joy?" Sitting in my "Holy Spirit" chair, my feet on the ottoman watching the birds on my patio fighting over the feeder, I thought, "This brings me joy!" And I began a list of all that brings me joy:

- Watching the birds
- Doing my word puzzles
- A picture of my daughter with her grandbabies
- Seeing pictures of my grandkids and their families
- My pets
- My meetings and the women I look forward to seeing there
- Cheering for my favorite teams
- Taking a nap without guilt whenever I want to
- Reading
- Writing

My list just keeps growing. It makes me want to encourage others to see what their personal histories could mean to them. We all have a story. When we view our true story with honest, open, and willing minds, much healing can take place. We can see where life takes us, with thanksgiving.

Where can your story take you? How can your story help others in their life journeys?

Mine has taken me to a joyful, free, and happy present despite all the mistakes that I made along the way!

Do I have any regrets?

You betcha!

I wish that I had had the courage to make a safer world for my children as they were growing up! God knows my heart and has forgiven me, as His Word tells me, "as far as the east is from the west."

How could we ask for anything more?

9 781948 382120